Real
Barnsley

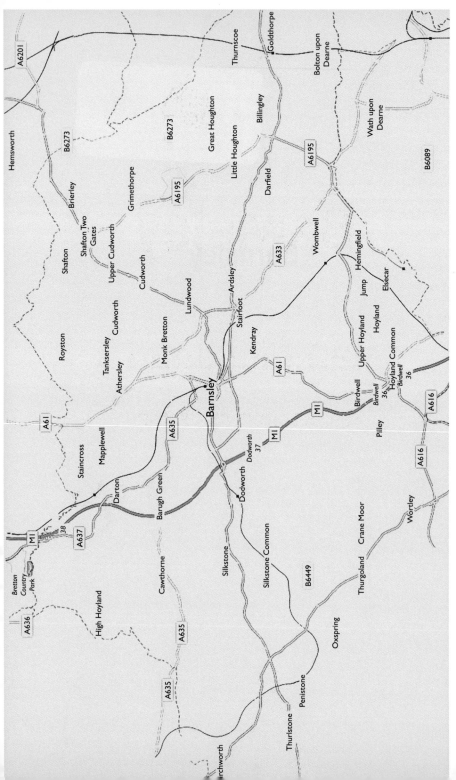

Real
Barnsley

Ian McMillan

SERIES EDITOR: PETER FINCH

Seren is the book imprint of
Poetry Wales Press Ltd
Nolton Street, Bridgend, Wales

www.serenbooks.com
facebook.com/SerenBooks
Twitter: @SerenBooks

ISBN 978-1-78172-411-8

A CIP record for this title is available from
the British Library

The publisher works with the financial assistance
of the Welsh Books Council

Cover photography: © Craig Skinner,
www.craigskinnerphotography.co.uk

Printed by Latimer Trend & Company Ltd, Plymouth.

CONTENTS

SERIES EDITOR'S INTRODUCTION

The Barnsley I might have expected to visit – 70 working coal pits, glassmakers, wire and linen mills, a huge Co-op, and Barnsley Chops being consumed on every street corner – is no more. It has been replaced by the bright new Barnsley of the twenty-first century future. This is one of clean streets and high-rise glittering glass. One where the depression of industry's long decline has at last given way to vibrant optimism. In fact the first impression of any visitor to the centre of this rural conurbation of ten towns and twenty-three villages is of the way that the new strikes bold amid the past of King George and Queen Victoria.

The centre of the Metropolitan Borough of Barnsley, which is what this great Yorkshire east of the Pennines scattering is formally known as, is naturally Barnsley itself. *Berneslai* as the Domesday Book listed it and still pretty much sounding the same. Its early rise as the crossing point of the routes from Sheffield to Wakefield, Rotherham to Huddersfield and Cheshire to Doncaster is apparent at the rail and bus station to the east of town. Here Barnsley has been given some futuristic wrap-around bridges, a video screen information system and re-named Barnsley Interchange. The walk into town takes five minutes. In fact the walk right across town, east to absolute west doesn't take much longer. Central Barnsley – pubs, shops, parks and hills – you can contain in one afternoon. Bigger Barnsley, the one of the scattered towns of Grimethorpe, Darfield, Elsecar, Jump, Royston, Wombwell and the rest takes a little longer.

In the days of coal this place was an industrial epicentre. The local economy of coal was dominant. It was a workers town. But nothing lasts. In the years after the miners' strike of 1984-85 the National Union of Mineworkers established their HQ here to fight the decline. Arthur's Castle, as it was locally known, is an ornate turreted Victorian masterpiece at the top end of town. Slogans still adorn it. Coal not Dole. Justice Delayed Justice Denied. Arthur Scargill is a local although there doesn't seem to be a Civic Trust blue plaque that tells me so.

Elsewhere central Barnsley is a paradise of memorials – plaques, lamppost banners, statues and notices mark out the famous wherever you look. The faces of comedians Harry Worth, and Charlie Williams along with singer Kate Rusby hang over Midland Street. There are plaques to Joseph Locke, civil engineer, and then another at the spot where his father once lived. The building in which missionaries to China, James and Elizabeth Taylor, might have met John Wesley is marked as is the place where the chapel built by James Taylor's grandfather once stood. There's a statue of cricket umpire Harold 'Dickie' Bird by local sculptor Graham Ibbeson. This is on a plinth near the offices of the *Barnsley Chronicle*. The plinth is a recent addition. It has been provided to prevent inebriated locals from hanging rude items on the statue's outstretched finger.

Other famous locals, so far without plaque as far as I can tell, include the broadcasters Jenni Murray and Michael Parkinson, along with the poet and author of the current splendid Real book, Ian McMillan. But it's only a matter of time.

Opposite Dickie Bird's statue is a recently unveiled memorial to the three hundred and eighty-three miners who died in the Oaks Colliery explosions of 1866. In the Victorian era pit safety was the least of the owner's concerns. The Oaks disaster was the largest in British history until that at Senghenydd in 1913 surpassed it. Ibbeson is again the sculptor. Woman and child rushing pitwards for news with a miner clawing the ground beneath them. The pit itself was not far away from here in what is now the Dearne Valley Country Park.

The Cooper Gallery on Church Street was originally the 1769 home to Barnsley Grammar School. When that school moved on, art collector and local benefactor Samuel Cooper bought the site. The building and his collection of European masterpieces, Turner to Wadsworth, he subsequently left to the people. Here are landscapes and faces from a long past I'll never witness. On special show when I visit are Anton Want's photographs, *Remnants of Change*, depicting recent social and structural changes within the town. You can see Barnsley shifting before your eyes.

Unlike much of Barnsley's soft and yellow millstone grit the Town Hall has been constructed of a more authoritarian Portland Stone. In its pursuit of power and strength it resembles the Parliament Building at Stormont in Northern Ireland. No surprise. The architect, Sir Arnold Thornely, is the same. Approaching it up Regent Street, its dominance is resolute. George Orwell, in Barnsley at the start of the 1930s depression researching his *The Road To Wigan Pier*, thought the money spent on this structure a total waste. It should instead have been given to starving miners.

The Town Hall has a field of fountains, a traditional war memorial and some unmistakably modern sculpture in its forecourt

(Nigel Hall's *Vertical* of 2006). Everything is dazzlingly floodlit at night. On an upper floor the Mayor has allegedly installed a sunbed. Here too are the galleries of Experience Barnsley, a local museum and interpretation centre. This wonderland of Barnsley history and artefact takes a whole afternoon to encompass. Inside illuminated and carefully annotated cases are miners' lamps, a LNER London 1939 Day Excursion poster, Arthur Bower's giant wooden football rattle, an early Barnsley Swimming Club trophy, Mrs Atkinson's Gas Mask, Neolithic flint daggers, Bronze Age spear heads, fossil ferns and fossil tree roots. In addition there is the first Purple Ronnie greetings card, composed by local poet Milly Johnson in 1980. In the next case is a Sooty Junior Xylophone manufactured

by Arthur Greenwood's Green Monk Toys in Darfield. High spot for me is the plate that celebrates the eight feet by four feet collier's pie baked to raise money for Wombwell Hospital in 1938. I get the feeling that Barnsley past was a joyous place.

Not that the present is bad. On a walk down the gently sloping hill to the Market and the Alhambra Shopping Centre people nod and smile. That air of alienation present in the heart of so many cities is absent here.

Barnsley is a place of knowledge. This is made clear by the University and Further Education tower blocks, most of recent construction, which interleave throughout the centre. Young people are everywhere. Tattoo parlours. Street art. Skateboards. Bars.

Restaurants that implore you to take the challenge. At the Grill Pit they offer Man vs Food, Glutton or Incinerator. What will you get? Fame or shame. Ask inside.

The Barnsley Chop, a double-sized slab of loin of lamb, which ought to be a fixed item on all menus is strangely lacking. Barnsley Chops were served to guests at the 1933 opening of the Town Hall, by the Prince of Wales, but they've been thin on the ground since. They do, however, remain as a house special on the menu at one of the places with a claim on their invention, the Brooklands Restaurant out near the M1.

Outsiders' impressions of Barnsley, mine included, often stem from the films that made the place famous. Ken Loach's 1969 *Kes* was made in Barnsley villages while his *The Price of Coal* (1977) was set in the fictional Milton Colliery nearby. *Brassed Off*, set in the early 1980s, was filmed in Grimethorpe. The brass band tradition here is still strong.

The workless world depicted in those films has been replaced. Mega online young person's clothing retailer ASOS has their fulfilment centre here. The largest cake bakery in Europe, Premier Foods, make Mr Kipling Cakes in Carlton. There are kitchen, double glazing and joinery manufacturers. And there's a bottle maker, Ardagh Glass, creating new product but still offering a connection with the past.

Out at Elsecar, reached by train through green countryside but still Barnsley, stands the Elsecar Heritage Centre. This is the Earl Fitzwilliam's ironworks and colliery village reborn as a living museum. At weekends steam trains run from a refurbished stuck-in-1930s-aspic station, signals, tracks, and rows of steam engines in the process of restoration. There's a canal lined with fishermen, workshops, a reservoir (known locally as Elsecar-on-Sea), a bandstand and the only Newcomen mine shaft Steam Beam Engine (1787) still operating anywhere in the world. These things pulled water from the depths and pumped in air. At the interpretation centre I watch films from the 1950s showing Elsecar in the last gasps of its dirty industry. The beam engine banging and the world full of noise.

Outside I wander among the cafés and ironwork chimneys. In the antique market are stalls retailing Roman coins, Saxon brooches and the rusty finds of local detectorists. Alongside are traditional sweet shops, children's clothes retailers, a letterpress printer, and then, amazingly, a whole vinyl record store, Vinyl Tap. This retails

the past as if it were still the present. Seven inch singles, EPs, twelve inch albums. Rock and roll to punk, Frank Sinatra to progressive rock, psychedelia, and thrash. All returned to splendour.

The museum is one of a run of eight maintained by the council right across the Barnsley Metropolitan region. Entrance to everything is free, opening times tight (open late, close early) and timekeeping vaguely southern Mediterranean.

Barnsley is a post-industrial place from which the grime has completely vanished. Unlike many such regions that feeling of workless desperation, dope and drunkenness is harder to find. The town has looked forward. It ran a consultation called *Rethinking Barnsley* in 2002 and then delivered on the results. The fresh apartments, cultural provisions, digital media centres, and other regenerations are gleamingly evident. It's a new Yorkshire world.

Ian McMillan has made it his life's work to keep the name Barnsley in front of the public. I first came across him while I was editing the literary magazine *second aeon* in the 1970s he was a Barnsley poet. He still is. The Bard of Barnsley. He is the only poet I know to have been both resident at the local football club (Barnsley F.C., east of the rail station, walk down Bala Street then Belgrave Road) and at Humberside Police HQ where he became their beat poet. He was born in the town and still lives here. He knows Barnsley's foreways, sideways and byways like no other. The perfect author for a Real book.

Peter Finch

WELCOME

Welcome to this walking and talking map of Barnsley; in it, I've followed the traditional format of this series by looking at North and East and West and South and Central but, as I wandered about, I realised (and I bet I'm not the only author of these Real books to notice this) that these divisions become increasingly artificial the more you dive into a place and swim around in it, occasionally coming up for air.

For a start, various tropes and scenarios repeat themselves across the borough: here is the village that was a sleepy rural backwater until somebody found coal on the master's land and rushed up to the big house to tell him as he nodded over his devilled kidney breakfast in the dining room. The most exciting thing that had happened in the previous year was that Hodge had dropped a turnip and it had rolled haphazardly into the pond. Now the villagescape was about to change forever. This play is performed over and over and again across Barnsley; sometimes the big house survives, sometimes it is turned into apartments, sometimes it has fallen into disrepair.

Over the late nineteenth and early twentieth centuries people rushed into Barnsley from all over the place and the town and the villages around it expanded rapidly; streets and streets of houses were built and church and chapel and pub and cinema and theatre congregations and audiences boomed. The older things were sat on by the newer things and they grew or they were subsumed. Churches that had been in the middle of a field for years were suddenly surrounded by houses. The fields themselves, with their ancient tangible and intangible patterns, were covered by layers of modernity. Railways and canals and roads brought noise and money from one place to another and then took noise and money from another place to another.

Coal reigned supreme. Glass was blown and linen was stretched across fields catching the drying light of the sun but everywhere the landscape was full of turning pit wheels. The slipstream of the mining industry, its brass bands and choirs and buses and football teams and cricket teams and tiny factories making things that they might use down the pit filled the place to bursting, sonically and visually.

At the northern and western edges of all this frenetic digging, some things didn't change: because there was no coal to be dug up, the farming carried on. Sometimes, in a D.H. Lawrence kind of way, the farming carried on anyway, with lowing cattle being driven across railway lines just after a clanking coal train had lumbered almost endlessly by. These two worlds rubbed against each other uneasily and there was a sense that this co-habitation would never end. Indeed I often quote the piece of writing I did at primary school called 'Barnsley in the Year 2000', where I said that we would all wear silver suits and eat our dinner in tablet form and go to the pit on a silver monorail rather than in one of Camplejohn's buses. In other words, the pit would be there forever.

And, of course, it wasn't. The miners' strike of 1984-85 and the shutting down of the coalfield have reverberated in this area ever since. I liken it to a huge gong, struck hard, deafening us all for a long time; the reverberations are still going on but we're starting to be able to hear other things, faintly. They're getting a little louder. The smoke, to bring another image into the mix, is starting to clear a bit and we're emerging, blinking, into the harsh light. We are looking backwards and forwards at the same time: we're reclaiming history and we're trying to reinvent ourselves as a place and as a population. Perhaps the same tale, with slight variations, is being told in all the parts of the borough where the mines were. Perhaps my job as a writer is to note and celebrate nuance. Perhaps your job as a reader is to note and celebrate it alongside me.

So as well as the topographical wanderings in the book I'll be writing what Eugene O'Neill might have called Strange Interludes; they'll take me across the borough and they'll take me back in time and back inside my head. Think of them as poemy things.

Around Barnsley I'm easily spotted. I'm the one with the notebook.

EAST

TO DARFIELD MUSEUM

It's Saturday morning and my wife and I leave the house and stroll down to Darfield Museum, or to give it its extended gobfull of a title 'The Maurice Dobson Museum and Heritage Centre'[1] because it's time for our monthly volunteering stint. This isn't a strictly local point, but I'm intrigued that you walk 'Down Darfield' even though you don't descend anything, and 'Up Wombwell' even though you go down a hill before you ascend one.

In the museum I meet and greet, stand behind the counter in the shop and guide people around, and my wife serves in the café with Pauline, a serial volunteer and stalwart of the committee, toasting pikelets and slicing cake. Recently, after many years of negotiating with various council bodies with clipboards in their hearts, we had brown signs erected to direct people to the museum; our joy was slightly rusted by the fact that one of the signs faced the wrong way, guiding people to the bus shelter, but in the end we agreed that all publicity is good publicity, and the sign was eventually rotated by a different collective of clipboard warriors.

We pass the chip shop, the Cricket Club, the Conservative Club, which was formerly a Wesleyan Chapel, Darfield All Saints Junior School and the houses built on the site of the old Green Monk toy factory. When I was a boy playing in the local park[2] with a couple of lads whose faces are hazy because they became Ten Pound Poms, you could smell the paint they used at the toy factory as it hung over the village like a scarf. An old bloke once looked up from his seat by the swings and said, in a voice like a squeaky gate, 'Smells like they're mekkin xylophones this morning'.

On the corner, by the Cross Keys and across from All Saints Church where I used to ring bells for weddings (three quid a rope) and funerals (half-muffled clappers for dignity and remembrance), is the white-walled museum. We open at 10.00am and my first job will be to put the heavy green metal advertising A-board out. It seems to weigh more every week. Must be all that history.

When anybody asks, and even when they don't, I tell them that Darfield Museum is the only establishment in the world named after a gay cross-dressing ex-marine, although Elsie, who also works in the museum shop and the museum café told me he was actually in the Scots Guards, but somehow that seemed less euphonious even if it was true. The man in question is the eponymous Maurice

Dobson; he was born in Low Valley, between Darfield and Wombwell in 1912, worked briefly down Darfield Main Pit[3], joined the Royal Marines/Scots Guards and then worked in service in a number of hotels called the Grand, according to the postcards he sent home. Maurice and his partner Fred were that very unusual phenomenon in a mid-twentieth-century pit village, an out gay couple who didn't care what people thought about them and their lifestyle choice.

My mother used to talk about seeing both of them dressed in summer frocks and elaborate, almost neon, make-up walking hand in hand down the lane to Houghton Main[4]. In my imagination they would pause briefly to make daisy chains to garland each other with. They ran the building that's now the museum as a corner shop and off-licence with a beer pump on the counter and, because they were both military men, responded to any homophobic abuse from lads on their way to the youth club at the church hall with a clip round the ear. Maurice would sit in state on a high stool smoking a cigarette and wearing a powder blue suit and a cravat like a hanging basket. He would turn to me and one of the aforementioned proto-Ten Pound Poms and say in his Kenneth-Williams-in-South-Yorkshire tones 'If you say bugger I'll give you a Spangle' and Fred, sombre in his brown smock, would shake his head ruefully and carry on sweeping the clean floor.

Maurice collected militaria and antiques and towards the end of his life he decided to donate his house, an old Georgian one, to the community as a museum. Like all such grand gestures, made with the aid of a waved cigarette in a holder making a circle of fire in the air, it was much easier said than done. Eventually, though, with the help of local councillors and the hardworking Darfield Amenities Society, endless meetings in a succession of rooms and money from trusts and the National Lottery, the museum opened at Easter 2001 as the new millennium got its feet under the table and dosh from John Major's pet project fluttered over post-industrial sites like confetti.

My wife goes into the café ready for the first visitors who will probably include Dennis, the man who used to run a bus company, and the chap who has a flat-green bowling green in his back garden. I check out the two upstairs rooms that are the heart of the museum, just to make sure that nothing has fallen off. One of the rooms celebrates the mining, of course, that was the heart (now the broken heart) of the industry round here, but also Darfield's smaller industries, the toy factory and the Mitre Football Factory.

The football factory used to be halfway up Snape Hill and in a case at the museum we've got a fearsome implement that the women who worked at Mitre Sports used to have to grip between their knees as they put the footballs together. In a separate case there's one of the xylophones they made at the Green Monk toy factory and the sight of it recalls the smell of it and the old man in the park. Arthur Greenwood, the man who ran the factory, was a visionary and an inventor with over a hundred patents to his name; he designed an all-seater football stadium years before they became the norm; his stadium would have held 250,000 people, which is exactly the number of people who claim they were at Oakwell in April 1997 to see Barnsley beat Bradford City 2-0 to win promotion to the Premier League. The toy factory closed in 1984, when it felt like the rest of Darfield was closing around it.

A couple come into the museum; they've heard about us from our website and I show them around, lingering over the tales of Maurice, skating over the historical facts I'm not that clear about because history is fiction written by the winners anyway, as they say.

My favourite display is our case of mystery objects; I take them out with a flourish and ask the visitors to guess what they are and they fall at the first hurdle, the rectangular piece of wood with the spots on like a first draft of a dice. The man thinks it's a child's game. The woman thinks it's something to with maths. The man thinks it's a form of notation for a musical instrument. The woman gives up. The man gives up. They seem slightly underwhelmed when I tell them it's a device used by railwaymen in the early twentieth century to test their eyesight. Still, I know they'll enjoy the toasted teacake in the café; you can see the currants in there as clear as day.

CHURCHYARD

I walk past Darfield Museum and through the churchyard to get to the old part of the village called Millhouses. This is where I used to walk as a lad with my mates on our endless evening circuit looking for what I guess we loosely defined as Life. Sometimes we clutched chips and mushy peas from the Inkerman Road fish shop. Sometimes we clutched cans of pop from Mrs Batty's shop. Our rebellion was a cosy one that was so innocent it could probably have been played on *Children's Favourites* with Uncle Mac.

From the museum you can glance to the left and see the old Reading Room, opened in the nineteenth century and now a private house. Reading Rooms were common in the early 1800s before the spread of public libraries, and older people in Darfield have told me how they remember sitting in there to read the daily papers. In my memory it was used as a store for builder's materials, where you could go and read a bag of cement if you wanted. Concrete poetry.

The Cross Keys pub is a newer version of the old Cross Keys which was demolished in the middle of the twentieth century; next door to the pub was an ancient factory belonging to the organist at the church, Ernest Wiley. I worked there many weekends and summer holidays, hanging Stanley knives on wires for a man called Dick to paint. One of the lads who worked there once fell asleep and, in an action that was probably as old as the idea of steel toecaps, we welded his toecaps to a piece of heavy metal and then told him the factory was on fire. Oh, how we laughed.

Pass Darfield Church Hall, which always looks, with its wide, flat frontage, as though it should be in Tombstone. The reason for this unusual architecture is that it was the Empire Cinema until December 1956; inside, you can still get the feel of how it was as a cinema, and I always marvel at the way whole villages would pack into these palaces of delight in their hundreds, sitting through the same film twice unless the manageress caught you by the blazer lapels and gave you the bum's rush.[5] The Church Youth Club met there on a Monday night and the girl who is now my wife of many decades and I bonded there over snooker and table tennis.

One of the first times I ever stood up in public was at Darfield Church Hall, or rather, one of the first times I sat down in public. As the drummer with Darfield's first folk-rock band, Oscar the Frog, I was given the job of persuading the Mothers' Union committee to let us play at one of their jumble sales. They agreed after some pressure from Mrs Parry. It wasn't an auspicious showbiz debut: at a signal from me, Mr McCardle opened the curtains and we played twenty long minutes of jigs, reels and ballads to a crowd of women and children who appeared to be looting trestle tables before the imminent arrival of armed police. After twenty minutes Mr McCardle shut the curtains again and the clothing and bric-a-brac riot carried on.

I wander into the churchyard glancing left towards the beautiful old Darfield Rectory, site of the church garden party when I was a child; it's an austerely functional house that always resonates for me with the kind of aching beauty associated with lost childhood. The churchyard has been cleaned up and beautifully maintained over many years by the Friends of Darfield Churchyard, yet another suburban militia with public service in their hearts and black sacks and garden tools in their hands.

The churchyard is a fascinating repository of all kinds of dead; there's Robert Milthorp, who 'inadvertently threw this stone upon himself whilst in the service of his master' and so the master said 'well, stick it on top of him as a lesson to others!' I made up the

master's words but I bet he said something like that. There's Emily Wraith, who was brought back from Harvard College where she died of appendicitis; she was working for the wealthy Vanderbilt family at the time, and it was they who paid to bring Emily home. There's Henry Cross, who was a drover from Lincolnshire who just happened to be taken ill as he passed through Darfield in 1787 with his cattle, and he died.

Of course, because this is a mining area there are mining disaster memorials, including the one for the Lundhill disaster of 1857 in which 157 men and boys lost their lives, and for the lesser-known Houghton Main disaster of 1886 when the cage taking men to the bottom of the shaft fell in twelve seconds rather than three minutes, killing all ten men on board. When I was a boy there was a rumour that escaped convict Harry Roberts was living in an open grave and buying fish and chips in the School Street chip shop. Around the same time when the church clock began to slow down and make an odd sound like asthmatic breath, a number of locals were convinced (yes, including me) that it was the sound of a giant owl just waiting in the tower to come and snatch a babby from its pram. It wouldn't have mattered because Harry Roberts would have got it.

The interior of All Saints' Church is sumptuously lovely, a fact that I'm only just beginning to appreciate after having to sit there twice every Sunday to listen to interminable sermons and attempt not to wince at some of the contralto warbling that threatened the already subsidence-struck walls. Mind you, those Morning Prayers and Evensongs and psalms half-sung to the sound of Ernest Wiley's organ gave me a lifelong love of rhythmic language and of the all-pervading mystery that happens when music meets words in a resonant space. My mate Noel Marsden once tried to hypnotise me by swinging his dad's pit watch in front of my chubby face and the reverend Howard shouted from the pulpit 'We don't hypnotise people in church, young man!'

The church goes back to the twelfth century but was built on the site of an older Saxon church that dated from the eighth century; high in the walls on either side of the chancel you can see (well, I couldn't until I had them pointed out to me but now I can) Saxon stones from the original building. A learned man, visiting the church to look at the stones as part of an open weekend, noticed my puzzlement as I gazed at them and he pointed out that they wouldn't have been up there, high on the walls, originally; they'd have been placed there as part of building and rebuilding work.

There's an alabaster tomb of a knight and his lady who apparently have no connection with the parish and were brought there in the reign of Henry VIII from Beauchief Abbey in Sheffield for safekeeping; I'm sure Noel Marsden told me it was Sir Perceval Cresacre and his wife but I was probably hypnotised at the time. There's a huge, fascinating oak chest in the chancel with the faint traces of seven locks which would have needed a key from each of the seven villages that made up the former parish before it could be opened, which gives you some idea of Darfield's importance as a settlement in the Dearne Valley and beyond.

There's also a memorial window to Charles Malin Clifton Sorby, who was killed in the First World War and who lived at the rectory; his father, Canon Sorby, was the rector there. The beautiful brass plaque under the window tells us that Sorby was killed in action near Ypres on the 8 May 1915 'having just rescued his wounded sergeant under heavy shell fire'. The wooden cross that marked his wartime grave has been brought home and is fixed to the wall of the church, its simplicity contrasting with the majesty of the window.

My favourite parts of the church these days are the Jacobean box pews, three hundred and fifty years old and with the original butterfly hinges and bolts, the doors worn smooth by generation after generation of hands opening then and closing them and resting against them to gain purchase to stand up to sing.

To walk down, past the grave of the Corn Law Rhymer Ebenezer Elliott, and gaze across the flood plain of the River Dearne below, is to get a glimpse of what the view might have been when, at the time of the Domesday Book, Darfield was a place near a river where deer lived. Derefeld eventually became Darfield, as we were told endlessly at Low Valley School; our teachers were inordinately proud of the age of the village, though as kids we'd rather talk about the old air raid shelters in the school yard because as far as we were concerned they were just as old.

I make my way carefully down the churchyard steps and cross the park at the bottom of Pinfold Lane. The Thaal Indian restaurant, whose venison curry is second to none, used to be the Bridge Inn, which was my wife-to-be and my watering hole when we'd outgrown the church youth club. Of course the Bridge Inn that we sat and sipped halves of Barnsley Bitter and glasses of Cinzano and lemonade in was actually the new Bridge Inn because there was a fifteenth-century inn on the site that was demolished (here's a familiar clause in a sentence) in the 1960s. At least the old Bridge Inn was suffering from subsidence and not from the kind of formica modernism that convinced people that smashing pianos and feeding them through toilet seats was a good idea, as they did in that decade.

I cross the River Dearne and walk towards the section of Darfield known as Millhouses; on your right there are some new houses on the site of the old Toll Bar Fish Shop that used to be a toll bar. The road from Doncaster to Barnsley used to be an old salt route from Cheshire to North Yorkshire and on the Doncaster side of the river there was a toll booth which in later years became a café and a chip shop. There was a list of tolls on the side which was relocated to the site of the bowling club pavilion in the park. The café burnt down a number of years ago and a further link to the past was lost.

Millhouses has some unusual three storey houses, common on the steep streets of West Yorkshire but more unusual in South Yorkshire. The mill that the houses are named after was by the river and it's said that the monks from Monk Bretton Priory sailed down the river to get their corn. This is also the site of Darfield station, which was opened in 1840 and closed in 1963. Just as the road turns, by the site of the old bridge which was removed in the 1990s, you can see the steps up to the platforms. One of my earliest memories, which may simply be one of those events you've been told about so often that they become a memory, is of running up those steps with my mother to catch the first of a number of trains that would take us down to Plymouth to meet up with my dad leaving his ship, *The Ark Royal*, for the last time as he retired from the navy. Except... he retired in 1958 and I was born in 1956. So do I recall it? Do I recall sitting under that table in that hotel in Plymouth playing with my toy cars and talking nineteen to the dozen and somebody saying 'one day that boy will be Prime Minister of England'? I don't really know the answer to that, but every time I pass those station steps I can hear my mother's heels clacking.

At the side of where the station was is the old Station Inn, now the Mumbai Lounge, Darfield's second Indian Restaurant, opposite a suite of fine stone houses.

THE BRIDLE PATH

There are places in Barnsley that can take me on a stroll through the recent and distant past. At times I can come across history that is so close I can feel the stink of it, and at times I feel that if I peer really closely at the mist, a Roman soldier might take my hand.

I walk down Saltersbrook Road in Darfield until I come to the roundabout known locally as the Ring. For years, because of this local locution, I thought that roundabouts were ring roads and vice versa, and I still sometimes have difficulty linguistically distinguishing the two. At the Ring, Saltersbrook Road becomes Doncaster Road, and I get a sense that other boundaries are crossed there too. Salt was brought up this road from the mines of Cheshire and distributed to the towns around here; there's evidence of massive Roman settlements in Darfield and a hoard of coins was found in the late 1940s when building work began on a street that became known as Quern Way because they were found in a Quern.[6] A number of the streets round there are named after councillors and other politicians (Clarney Avenue, Morrison Road) and sometimes after their wives (Maran Avenue, named after the lovely Margaret Ann). For years the coins were kept across the border in Doncaster Museum but now most of them are back where they belong, in the new Experience Barnsley Museum in town.

I turn left down the Bridle Path and follow the route that thousands of miners would have taken to Houghton Main Colliery and Dearne Valley Drift Mine. The path is on a gentle slope down to the River Dearne and on my left are the high walls of Middlewood Hall, the house that's now divided into apartments but was once the home, in the late nineteenth and early twentieth centuries, of the self-styled Squire Taylor, who, although he was only the owner of a linen mills, definitely saw himself as part of some amorphous new-money branch of the landed gentry.

In the museum in Darfield we have copies of the card he had printed to invite people to his gymkhanas and a photo of him looking very much the squire, gazing into the middle distance that was the colour of money. The wall of the hall is so high that I'm convinced he had it built to such an elevation so that he couldn't see the little miners in their flat caps carrying their snap tins to the pit that generated bags of lifestyle for the friends he met for lunch at the Royal Hotel in Barnsley, in the same way that Harewood House near Leeds was dotted with trenches to keep the workers out of view of the moneyed. Amazingly (to me, anyway) there's at least one holiday cottage[7] with an indoor swimming pool in the complex of houses and conversions that are scattered around the hall; sometimes I fantasise about booking myself into it just to get a different view of Darfield, one with a view through steamed, misted glass.

The Bridle Path snakes down following the wall and crosses the River Dearne as it makes its way towards where Houghton Main pit used to be. When I was a teenager walking down the Bridle with my future wife, a rough boy shot at us with an air rifle and in my memory the pellet whizzed by my ear, although it probably didn't, really. That tale of marksboyship reflects the idea that the Bridle Path has always been a place of adult pursuits, of torches glinting in the night, of bikes loaded with something or other trundling into the darkness, of blokes with dogs and nets. There's a plum tree halfway down and, as my Uncle Charlie once said: "If only those plums could talk".

For years there was a rumour that a mandrake, a plant that screams when you pick it, grew down there; when I was a teenager Mark Smales said his dad had seen it as he walked down the path to start his shift at the pit. He also said, and here his voice trailed to a whisper, 'that he saw it in a different place every day' which led some sceptical lads to disbelieve the tale and made some gullible lads like me believe it all the more.

Houghton Main, at the end of the Bridle Path, was a behemoth of a pit with a railway line running by it carrying endless coal trains that made you think you were living in some flat American state where the freight trains didn't shift through the air, but simply *were*. On weekends, when services were diverted for engineering works, named trains would trundle by and me and my mates would gather by the fence to write the numbers down. Once, the Thames-Clyde Express trickled past. Memory may have distorted this vision, but I'm sure I recall a dining car full of toffs stopping to let the gasping engine steam into the frosty air. I saw a chef in a hat taller than the best Yorkshire pudding serving a man with a face like the later Auden's. Me and the gang waved like extras from *Kes*. The chef's ladle gleamed. The train began to saunter away. The man raised two meaty fingers at us in a gesture of contempt and class conflict. We ran home, excited and frightened.

Houghton Main Colliery was opened in 1873 and closed in 1993; at its height it employed thousands of men who would make their way up and down the Bridle Path at all hours of the day and night. An elderly man called George once told me that if you leaned very closely to the ground near the Bridle Path you could hear the men working; as he told me this story that may or may not have been true, his old mate Jim walked by. George gestured to him with a raised fist: 'Utopia, kid?' he asked. Jim nodded 'Utopia, kid!' he replied.

CAT HILL

It sometimes seems to me that round here we live in a post-factual world, that emotion and memory and opinion and sheer fantasy count more than measurable things, which is odd because this place has been built on hard, solid facts like tonnage from pits and glassworks. This post-factual world is certainly in evidence at Cat Hill, a tiny bump, like a ridge in a carpet, on the fringes of Darfield and on the old road to Broomhill.

I want to look at the legend and then I'll examine the facts and then I'll waltz back to the legend. The legend tells us that, sometime in the Fifteenth century, Sir Perceval Cresacre was returning from the crusades and was hacking his way through the wildwood that wrapped itself around much of South Yorkshire like a headscarf. As his horse stumbled and whinnied through the thick roots and overhanging branches they got set upon by a wild cat which sensibly ignored the horse and went for Sir Perceval's fine aristocratic neck. It scratched him and drew blue-ish blood and Sir Perceval swung his sword at the whirling cat, connecting and slicing away one of the nine available lives. The cat and the man, often capitalised in the oral stories as The Cat and The Man, made their way towards Darfield, fighting all the time. Nobody is quite sure, and maybe it doesn't matter, why they came to Darfield, except that it was an old, old, settlement even then, with evidence of Romans and a little citation in the Domesday Book.[8]

At Cat Hill (not called Cat Hill then, of course. Just called the Hill.) they fought and fought. Imagine claws and swords glinting in the sun. Then, and I don't know why, they turned left and fought their way across to Barnburgh, an interesting village which is just outside the scope of this book therefore of no interest to us at all, and on the steps of the church The Man dealt The Cat a fatal blow. At this point the elderly and W.H. Auden-faced denizens of Barnburgh (outside the scope of this book) will tap the side of their nose, point to the steps of the church and say 'And you can still see the blood. There. And there…' by now you're turning away, keen to get back to Barnsley, but they tug at your sleeve, '…and there.' The smudge that's meant to look like blood looks like a faded cup-a-soup stain to you but you don't say anything although your cynical thoughts may be loud enough to be heard by passers-by.

That's the legend, but the story is so pervasive that everybody my age (I'm 61) and above knows that the hill is called Cat Hill. The reality, as is so often the case, is different, and like much of Barnsley's history, or the history of any small town, is tiny and incidental. In an article in the *Yorkshire Post*[9] from 2010, Colin Howes, the Keeper of Environmental Records at Doncaster Museum says that there are a number of problems associated with the tale, the main one being that the woods which the man/cat kerfuffle traipsed through may not in fact have been woods at all at that time, which is bad enough, but as the article goes on to say 'one thing that has puzzled a lot of people was whether there were ever any cats big enough to do this sort of harm in South Yorkshire. Wild cats were rare then, and now they are a very rare native species confined to remote parts of northern Scotland. But my research indicates that there certainly were large, wild cats roaming the area and they were considered enough of a nuisance to be hunted…and wild cat skins were traded in York right up until the nineteenth century.' The story could well be true, then, and that's good enough for me.

If anybody ever visits Cat Hill I recommend that you go there in the company of me and my mate Iain the Artist: we're the Darfield Left Bank, the Darfield Greenwich Village, and we've been obsessed with this little hill, this rise-with-attitude, for years, Iain making paintings and sculptures of it and me writing poems about it.[10] And putting it in books. It turns off the A635 just before the roundabout onto the Dearne Valley Parkway that can speed people from Grimethorpe and Cudworth to the M1 at Junction 36. Time moves slowly round here, and although the part of the road near Cat Hill was opened in 1992 (there's inevitably a plaque and a tiny pit wheel) we still call it the New Road.

Cat Hill was once a B-road that connected Darfield and Broomhill, and beyond to Wath-upon-Dearne and the Manvers coking plant that lit up the night sky all through my childhood. It's important to my sense of who I am because my school bus used to rumble down it and inevitably get held up by huge coal trains for so long that some pupils, the ones who had homework to hand in, would get out and walk. To the left of the road was the place where the NCB would stockpile coal, where my father-in-law went during the miners' strike to pick coal, watched by coppers gazing at us from minibuses and counting pound notes. 'I dun't know what we're gunner do if they do owt,' my father-in-law said, taking off his flat cap to reveal a severe case of cap-ring, 'because I can't run and tha can't feyt.' So we did the sensible thing: we carried on putting tiny pieces of coal into a sack that had once held pigeon corn.

In the later years of the last century the road was blocked off to allow the new road to scythe through the countryside and now it has a neglected air. To the right there are the remains of Darfield's sandstone quarry where the amateur archaeologist Stephen Seal found fossil plants in 1879. Just beyond the quarry is where Darfield station would have been until 1963, when it fell victim to the Beeching cuts, shovelling up so much of the railway infrastructure to put into a sack that might have once held pigeon corn.

Cat Hill flattens out to a narrow road that meanders down to the Broomhill Tavern and on to the Old Moor Bird Reserve.[11] It's odd that it holds so much history and narrative and storytelling because it is so tiny. Stand there at night, though, and I reckon you can still hear The Cat fighting The Man. Or that might just be the murmuring from the parked cars full of young people.

GREAT HOUGHTON

When you've lived somewhere all your life, certain places that you've always known are engraved on your mind as places of romantic meeting, of historical importance, of national and global significance even if, viewed from the outside, they're small ex-pit villages in a former coalfield.

For me, Great Houghton is one of those places. My mother came from there so it's literally the motherlode. It's Proust's Madeleine and it's Seamus Heaney's Omphalos, so please forgive me if my writing about Great Houghton has a more than usually rosy hue and is heavy with adjectives and adverbs and a kind of faux-poetry.

There are three settlements under consideration here; Great Houghton, Little Houghton and Middlecliffe, each fitting inside the other like a series of Russian dolls with pit helmets on.

I begin in the nearest one of these to Darfield, Middlecliffe, which I get to by walking from Darfield and down the winding Fitzwilliam Road which is known locally as Coal Pit Lane. My dad had two allotments down Coal Pit Lane because he always thought that one wasn't enough, although he was a middle-aged man and I was a grumpy teenager who would rather dig Captain Beefheart than dig soil. There are a number of large houses near the top of Coal Pit Lane and when I was a younger man a rumour swept the village that the drummer from Def Leppard was going to live there because he wanted somewhere to land his helicopter. Maybe all villages are awash with this kind of rumour from time to time; maybe they're the equivalent of those 'Queen Anne Slept Here' tales that pop up everywhere, as they do in Great Houghton. Perhaps we all need rock or real royalty to give our humble streets the mark of approval, to give our lives a kind of vicarious lustre.

Middlecliffe, is a junction with a couple of streets, a Working Mens' Club (still open as I write this) and a corner shop. The intriguing thing about Middlecliffe is that, in the popular imagination of the older population and on the name of a house opposite the shop, it is called Plevna. If you look Plevna up on a map of the world it turns out to be the site of a major battle in the Russo-Turkish war of 1877-78. This was a big battle in a major war but even I, with my limited historical knowledge, know that it didn't spread as far as the outskirts of Barnsley. Despite my extensive research I can't find a definitive reason for the folk-name except that I half-recall a conversation with a historian somewhere (this wouldn't stand up in a court of law) who said that temporary shanty towns for workers were often called Plevna and that there would have been such a place nearby for the sinking of Houghton Main pit and the nearby Dearne Valley Drift Mine, where my grandad worked when he wasn't mending shoes. I hope that explanation is true.

I walk down the lane from Middlecliffe to Little Houghton, where Houghton Main and its enormous muckstack once dominated the landscape; these days Little Houghton is a sleepy settlement, because there's no through road to Grimethorpe and beyond. When I was a boy the 13 bus, the slow, slow bus between Doncaster and Barnsley, would turn off when you thought you were nearly home and go down the lane from Middlecliffe to Little Houghton, then turn round and come back again. The bus was run by a local firm called LP Buses, run by the grandly-named Larratt Pepper and known locally as Lariat's Chariots because the people of Barnsley couldn't quite believe that somebody could be called Larratt.

There's a pit wheel and a memorial at the end of the lane, and if you squint hard you can just about make out where the pit used to be. Near the former pit, and protected by a fence, there's an old butter cross, a market cross that is a distant echo of the busy crossing and trading place that this would once have been; the silence since the pit shut in 1993 is almost deafening. And of course there's a new development called Buttercross Drive.

I meander on the footpath up to Great Houghton, and come into the village by the old church. The drive through Great Houghton was my dad's favourite Sunday afternoon outing in the days when driving very slowly for pleasure was a major social activity. My dad kept up a lyrical, almost surreal, running commentary on the trip, which took a route that never varied at all. As we drove through Houghton from the Middlecliffe end he would change gear from his preferred third to a chugging first, and say 'We are now entering Great Houghton, famous for its ducky

pond'. My mother would point to sites she remembered from her childhood: Jack Brooks the newsagent, the now-demolished Briers Buildings or 'Hell Square' as she often called it, and the Old Hall Inn, which was always accompanied by a muttered 'what a shame' from my mother and a 'Queen Anne slept there. She must have been tired' from my dad.[12]

Great Houghton is a linear village and, like most of the villages in the borough, was an old farming hamlet that grew and filled and bulged like a bodybuilder once the local pits were sunk. The reason my mother would say 'What a shame' as we drove by the site of the Old Hall Inn was that it burned down in the 1960s and was rebuilt later; the actual Old Hall was an Elizabethan hall, which perhaps these days would have been preserved. The oldest building in Great Houghton is the Parish Church of St Michael and All Angels, a tiny sandstone building on the top of the hill overlooking the valley to Darfield and beyond. It was built in 1650 as a private chapel as part of the Old Hall estate by Sir Edward Rodes, the High Sheriff of Yorkshire and an officer in Cromwell's army. It's an astonishing building, I think, with a quality of light inside that seems to filter from the past. The single bell in the tiny exposed frame tolled for my mother's funeral in 2007 and the wind blew hard and the combovers of the pallbearers flapped like fronds of seaweed in a storm. There's a simple dignity to the place that speaks to me deeply, and not only because of my personal connections to it.

I walk to the end of Great Houghton, before I come to the woods that I know as Houghton Woods and the map calls West Haigh Woods, and I arrive at the place where the buses turn. That should be capitalised, actually, because it's so important in my folklore and in the folklore of this part of Barnsley. The Place Where The Buses Turn. The buses turn left off the road and go behind a white cottage that my dad always used to say was 'the house where Dick Turpin slept on his epic ride to York on his mighty stallion Black Beauty.' Yes, I know it was Black Bess, and so did he. As a boy (and as a man in late middle-age, I have to admit, though to a lesser extent) I was obsessed with this house, with the idea of living on a little island surrounded by the churning water of turning buses changing gear at all times of day and night.

Our Sunday afternoon drive in my dad's Zephyr 6 with the registration number UHE8 would carry on to Brierley Crossroads where we'd buy an ice cream at Danny's Ice Cream Van, and then we'd retrace our steps, park in a layby near the woods, and go for a stroll. At the edge of the woods at the Brierley side there's Burntwood Hall, which has in recent times been a nursing home, but which was originally an eighteenth-century farmhouse extended by William Marsden into, as sources put it, 'a residence fit for a gentleman'. It was still in the hands of a local family until 1979, and there really is a tunnel (unlike many of the fake tunnels that pretend to worm their way under much of the land surrounding big houses) that goes under the road from the house to the kitchen garden opposite. The Marsdens landscaped West

Haigh Wood and the nearby Howell Wood, which has an ice house and ornamental ponds.[13] There were ponds once in West Haigh Woods but try as we might my brother and I could never find them, no matter how hard we looked. Mind you, we once buried a message in a bottle under the spreading roots of a tree and we couldn't find it the next Sunday; I think somebody had moved the tree.

After a local paper article in the late 1990s I'm known as The Bard of Barnsley, and at the Great Houghton side of the woods is the farmhouse where the other Bard of Barnsley lived for the last few years of his life. Ebenezer Elliott[14] was known as the Corn Law Rhymer and was a radical nineteenth century poet who was born in Masbrough in Rotherham and who is buried in Darfield Churchyard; he was essentially a nature poet who was brought to political activism by a need to highlight the plight of the working northern industrial towns. His poem 'A poet's epitaph' is stirring and moving in equal measure:

> Stop, Mortal: here thy brother lies
> The poet of the poor
> His books were rivers, woods and skies
> The meadow and the moor.
> His teachers were the torn hearts' wail
> The tyrant, and the slave
> The street, the factory, the jail,
> The Palace and the grave.

Elliott's own grave in Darfield Churchyard is surrounded by a formidable fence that rumour has it Sir John Betjeman was instrumental in having preserved because he was disappointed that souvenir hunters were coming and chipping bits off the stone. It'll come to all us bards, I guess, eventually.

LOW VALLEY

Let's put our cards on the table and get this straight from the start: Low Valley is not New Scarborough and New Scarborough is not Low Valley. Right, that's that then. We'll come to this dichotomy later. Let's stroll through Low Valley to get to Darfield.

I'll leave Wombwell on the B6096, walking past the site of the old Wombwell Central Station which was on the old South Yorkshire Railway company's line between Mexborough and Barnsley. The station closed in 1959 but the line was there for much longer, and indeed when I lived in Low Valley in the early 1980s I remember walking by the old station on a Sunday and seeing amazed passengers on a diverted train in East Coast livery, leaning out of windows taking photographs.

By the old railway you pass the Wombwell Sporting Association and the go-kart track which has been a source of buzzing and whizzing entertainment for more than forty years and which was once confusingly called the Dorothy Hyman Stadium just like the one a few miles away in Cudworth, the home town of the eponymous local Olympic silver medal winner. Dorothy's name was taken off the Wombwell Sporting Association circuit although it still appears as such in some publications which results in anxious karters having to race (literally/not literally) to Cudworth as though they are in some kind of regional final.

Between the go-kart track and Low Valley proper, before the yard that used to belong to Mr Tingle the ice cream man, there's a house that used to be the register office and was also, in my mother-in-law's memory, a place where people would queue to get welfare in the days before the welfare state. I asked her what the house was called. She thought for a moment and said 'The Big House at the bottom of the hill'. Makes sense. Nominative determinism is alive and well. It's actually called Blakeney House, as I noticed when I strolled by the other day.

The Valley is the valley of the River Dove, and although it's not a steep valley, the area known as Low Valley always felt separate and distinctive. To the left, as you walk towards Darfield, you would have seen the muckstack (in Scotland, a bing, which always seems more lyrical) of Darfield Main Pit, a mine which only closed in 1989 when it merged with Houghton Main. As a child I would walk through Low Valley to go to Wombwell Market on a Saturday morning to buy comics from the legendary comic stall with my mates. I could take or leave Batman and Superman but I really liked the more obscure heroes like The Flash and Metal Men. I fancied Platinum, to be honest, but she would never have looked at me because I was more like Lead. If you've never read The Metal Men you won't know what I'm on about but if you have you will.

Walking back alone once (Chris Allatt had had to go to the dentist) from Wombwell to Darfield with my comics under my arm I was approached by some lads. 'Haz tha got thi babby books?' one asked. 'They're DC and Marvel,' I said and I may as well have been telling him the Great Yarmouth tide times. He held up a copy of Metal Men by one corner as though it was infectious. I could have rescued Platinum but I was too scared. 'Metal Men?' he said, repeating the words several times until they lost all meaning. 'How can they be metal men? Anyway, one of them's a lass!' I grabbed the comic and ran back to Darfield as fast as I could as the lads threw lumps of coal at me that had fallen from the Home Coal wagon when it went over a bump.

The Valley, you see, it's always been a bit different and Valleyers are a separate breed. I should know. My wife of almost forty years is a Valleyer and proud of it. I carry on walking past the pub that used to be called the Miners Arms and was then called the Viking Bar, and was then called Thawley's, and is now a Premier Mini Market with a cash machine. This pub and the others that dot the road were built to slake the mighty thirsts of the people who worked at the pit and the brickworks, but by the time my wife and I got married in 1979 and moved into Low Valley the pubs were quieter, less like scenes from Tombstone Lil.

When the Miners Arms changed its name to the Viking Bar there was a bit of a local sensation because the rumour was that the owner had replaced the bar with a full-size Viking longship and that the barmaids were dressed as Viking maidens. Because I wanted this to be true I never went in, and now I wish I had.

Further through the Valley there was a pub called the New Station Inn which became my wife and I's favourite Saturday night haunt, mainly because the landlord, a man with quite a high voice, had a collection of keyrings stuck to the ceiling of the snug, so if the conversation ever petered out you could always point at keyrings and talk about them. This area, like most post-industrial areas, has gone through lots of changes and maybe you could chart them through its pubs. So the Miners Arms/Viking Bar/Thawleys/Premier timeline was replicated at the New Station Inn when it became, for no discernible reason, the Wat Tyler Inn, even though Wat was not a Valleyer and had never visited the area, and then the Low Valley Arms. It's since been demolished and houses have been built there, but part of me hopes that when the new owners dig their gardens they find a keyring in the shape of an erect penis or one from

Saltburn on Sea. Perhaps if they listen carefully they can hear the ghost of the old pea-and-pie man doing the rounds in his van, ringing his old school bell. It sounds like this should have been happening aeons ago but he still jingled his clapper in the early 1980s when my wife and I lived down Low Valley. Because we were recent ex-students we went out for the Saturday night pie and peas with a sense of irony, something that probably eventually killed off his trade. You can have mint sauce but irony dries the peas up.

As the road bends, at Scarborough Corner, you pass the site of the legendary, riotous streets that made up New Scarborough, that straddled the lane down to the Ings. Nobody really knows why it was called New Scarborough, even my mother-in-law, and she lived there for many years. There are a number of theories about the name. Possibly the area flooded a lot so it was as though the tide was coming in; perhaps it was an ironic reference to it being like a seaside resort. Maybe, and I admit I'm the only person who thinks this, the land was owned by the Earl of Scarborough. He could have won it in a game of cards when the port was flowing like, well, like the River Dove. New Scarborough mainly exists in the heads of people like my mother-in-law, who is in her eighties, because not a lot has been written about it. What she remembers is that the people of Low Valley regarded New Scarborough as rough, in the same way that the people of Darfield regarded the people of Low Valley as rough. I guess it's the same with the social gradations of Hampstead Garden Suburb.

The houses would have been built for the people who worked at Darfield Main pit and the nearby brickworks, and the children who lived in these houses would have been frightened to go to sleep because of the legend (or is it true? Press that button on this page of the book now that releases the frightening music) of The Valley Ghooast. The tale of the ghost that went around the Valley scaring people was celebrated in verse by the Darfield poet Billy McHale. I'm sad to report that the works of Billy, a man of great learning and gentle demeanour, have been lost to the world. There was a tiny book of his work published in the 1980s but I gave my copy away, and I can find no record of him on the internet. The Valley Ghooast reappeared in person, more or less, in 2006 when the landlord of the Low Valley Arms reported seeing an apparition that scared him to death. *The Star*, Barnsley edition, takes up the story: 'Landlord Roger Froggatt had confronted a ghostly woman in white with half her face missing. Roger was speechless with shock and his wife Kathryn called the police, believing he had confronted an intruder. Officers [press the scary music button again please] found no signs of entry, although the alarms had been tripped and all the TVs were turned on. Officers were left shaken and baffled by a toilet in the ladies, repeatedly flushing by itself.'[15] The ghost-hunter Darren Johnson-Smith said 'Usually I wouldn't be interested. There are lots of pubs that have their own ghosts. But the flushing of toilets witnessed by two police officers makes it.' The Valley Ghoooast is seemingly alive and well; Darren claimed, after some time performing what *The Star* called 'a meditation in the toilet' came up with a name for the ghost, Mary Quantrill and, like a valley version of Cluedo, decided that she was a nineteenth century traveller who'd been killed by a man with a hoe, on or near the site of the pub. A police spokesman, who had an Olympic silver medal in understatement, said 'Officers saw the toilet flushing but could not explain it.'

Round the corner from the New Station/Wat/Low, across Stonyford Road and the river, where Wombwell became Darfield there were three pubs, the George, the Bricklayers Arms and the Sportsman, of which only the Sportsman remains. The Bricklayers Arms was known locally as The Drop because there was a big step down into the bar, a trap for the unwary or the drunk. The George and the Drop have been demolished to make way for houses and the Sportsman carries on, at the Low Valley end of Pit Street which leads down to the site of the aforementioned Darfield Main.

I think that a stroll through this part of Barnsley is a microcosm of so many other parts of the borough: the agricultural, the industrial, the post-industrial all in the blink of history's watering eye. I remember when I was at Wath Grammar School, some of our school buses were going to be delayed, and a teacher from the South of England read out the list: 'Buses to Goldthorpe, Thurnscoe, Great Houghton (she pronounced it Huffton, to moughled giggling) and Low Valley. She looked around. 'What is wrong with that phrase?' she asked, her voice rigid with squeaky authority. 'Don't know miss,' somebody said. She smiled a superior smile and said 'All valleys are low. That's tautology. Can any of you spell it?'

WOMBWELL

Let's get the name out of the way first. Come on, just say it. Say it a few times and let's all get used to it. No laughing and giggling at the back. Wombwell. Wombwell. Wombwell. The O is short and tight, like Wumbwell. It's not Woooombwell, not at all. And yes, children, it's got the word womb in it. And yes, it's not too far from Jump. And yes, the Woodcock Travel Agency in Shafton mainly catered for the honeymoon trade. I'm always amazed at the number of people who find the name either hilarious or somehow transgressive and whisperable in the easily-shocked air.

The name probably comes from Womba's Well, or 'well in a hollow' and, like much of Barnsley borough, Wombwell is a palimpsest of layer upon layer of history. There was a Wombwell Hall, inevitably, that was demolished in the nineteenth century and there was a family called the De Wombwells who took their name from the place. It was a place of farming and small-scale, almost private, coalmining and then once the industrial revolution slapped the landscape round the chops it was overlaid with roads, railways and canals that still define the topography of the place. Wombwell, though. What a name.

I'll start walking into Wombwell town centre via Wombwell station from the back of Wombwell Woods, an ancient tract of land that includes a Romano-British settlement at a secret location that was so secret the bloke from Barnsley museums who was taking me to it couldn't find it and then stumbled upon it by accident when we were watching a bloke walk by with his dog. To stroll through Wombwell Woods is to seemingly be in the presence of timeless tree gods and timeless litter-worshippers, who pile the rubbish into detritus-cairns and altars to the sacred black sack full of wallpaper and chip pans and DVDs of forgotten Hollywood films.

Wombwell Woods or, to give it its official name, Wombwell Wood, envelops you as you walk through it. It was mentioned, like much of Round Here was, in the Domesday Book, and the ponds in the wood seems to reflect history along with the sky. Tales abound of the haunted nature of the woods, and intrepid locals and off-comed 'uns often scare themselves to death by looking for (and sometimes seeing: you decide) ghosts, although to my sceptical eye they could be just black sacks flapping in the breeze. The internet brims with stories of wood-spooks. One story goes that a couple were returning home from a night out in 1964 when a figure who looked like Guy Fawkes leaped out at them and *they drove straight through him*. There's a follow-up to this story from the 1980s where, according to the *South Yorkshire Times*, a student from Sheffield University was researching sightings of Guy Fawkes ghosts, but the internet poster goes no further. I've never seen Guy Fawkes or his ghost in the woods but maybe I've been looking at the wrong time of year.

In the nineteenth century there was a quarry in Wombwell Woods and there are rumours of a tunnel, sometimes known as the Convicts' Tunnel, because it was built by convicts from a local jail, or by Irish workers who were constructing the railway that passes close by. People claim that the tunnel is in many different areas of the wood, and that it's 'more of an underpass' and that it's boarded up, like many of the tales about it are.[16]

You emerge from Wombwell Woods and walk by the station that's now called Wombwell but was called Wombwell West to distinguish it from Wombwell Central, in the middle of town. For years, as you passed under the road bridge on the way to Sheffield, you'd pass a sign that said Let God In, which faded with time until a zealous atheist or a railway official following orders painted it out. Wombwell West opened in 1897 and the west was lost in 1967 although for years, until at least the turn of the new millennium, a sign on the old NatWest bank on Wombwell High Street pointed to Wombwell West. Rumours, like those of the drive-through ghost and the convicts' tunnel, washed around South Yorkshire that a train enthusiast with a set of steps and some bolt-cutters removed it one night and it's now got pride of place in his garage. Like Elsecar and Darton it's been an unmanned station for many years but I vividly remember my brother John taking a bike up there and loading it onto a train ready for a trip to the North Yorkshire Moors. I recall a station employee (was his huge moustache just in my mind and not on his face? Possibly) asking if he wanted the bike to go First or Second class and me and my brother and my dad not realising this was a joke.

Walk down Hough Lane past the site of the old foundry and the Wombwell Cricket Club; there was a greyhound stadium here until the early 1970s and I remember being taken there as a very young boy by my Uncle Charlie and his son Little Charlie. Little Charlie was smoking a cigar for some reason and I remember him taking it out of his mouth and saying to me, the words seemingly coming from the smoke, 'It's a real rabbit, tha knows. And I'll be having it for my supper later on, kid.' It must have been the smoke that made my eyes leak hot tears.

When I was younger, Wombwell was the place we went to do all our shopping, and although the High Street has seen better days, it's still got a number of independent shops that, if this was the trendy flank of West Yorkshire and not the glossed-over ribs of South Yorkshire, would attract hipsters and bohemians. Mills's DIY can get you any bucket in any size and a range of birdseed that would suit any flying thing from a hoopoe to Icarus. King's Bacon Shop does you black puddings that deserve to be a UNESCO World Heritage Site all on their own. And Potter's Butchers still make the best pork pies I've ever tasted, although I know that other pies, like those made by Dennis Speed or Percy Turner are available. Potter's have a combination of crust, meat and jelly that make you believe forever in the evolution of man from a gormless fish to an intellectual powerhouse of a human being. Of course, if you mention pork pies anywhere in the Barnsley borough, the name Albert Hirst will come bubbling to the surface.[17] Albert Hirst's pork pies, and his black puddings, and his sausage rolls, have taken on a legendary status since the last shop shut. You hear tell of cattle sent down by train from Edinburgh (First Class? You decide) and met at the old Court House Station by members of Hirst family in aprons and straw hats, and of 100 squealing pigs being driven through the town at midnight, waking children up who had to be calmed by anxious mams who did their best to reassure them it wasn't the Bogey Man or his plumper brother the Porky Man.

I was once doing some filming for local TV[18] in the Potter's Pork Pie factory on the High Street. They'd had me doing the 'poet tries to be part of the assembly line' scene and my humiliation was total and messy, as the women laughed me out of the room, as my pies piled up on the conveyor. Then we filmed the process of putting the meat into the crust and at one point, holding his hand up like a traffic cop, one of the Potters said 'Can we turn the camera off now, please? We can't show the secret ingredient'. In fact I'm sure he said it like this: *Secret Ingredient*, as though it was a code. My happiness was and is complete: a pork pie with a secret ingredient!

As a boy I recall that Wombwell was the place we went to for our shopping, rather than Barnsley, because there was no need to go any further. My mam and dad would get dressed up and we'd go in on an early Saturday afternoon after I'd been there in the morning with the lads. At Turvey's shop I'd buy even more triangular stamps for my collection of triangular stamps. At Diggles's department store we'd test settees for slumping potential. At Potter's we'd buy pork pies. There was a Burton's, a Boots, a Woolworth's, a Timothy White's and a Rediffusion shop where I bought singles and sometimes an LP or two. I don't want to sound nostalgic but there's no doubt places like Wombwell (and Cudworth, and Goldthorpe, and Thurnscoe) have seen better days and it would be hard now to buy triangular stamps in any of these locations. Like Goldthorpe, Wombwell has been by-passed by a bypass which means that any passing trade simply passes by. But I've always liked Wombwell's community spirit, an example of which is the Friends of Wombwell Cemetery[19] who, following increased vandalism in the cemetery in the early years of this century, have restored and catalogued many of the graves and have, most impressively, turned one of the chapels of rest into a community hub, a tiny beacon of life in the (forgive me) dead centre of Wombwell.

GOLDTHORPE

Along the A635 from Barnsley to Doncaster, once I've passed Cat Hill, I come to the Dearne towns of Goldthorpe, Thurnscoe and Bolton upon Dearne. Some people argue that Highgate is a separate place, and my memory of Highgate is the Halfway House pub, now demolished and apartmentalised where, on a Friday and Saturday night as a teenager, I could see all kinds of raw and enthusiastic rock bands[20]. I could stand far too close to the speakers so that my half of Barnsley Bitter trembled and shook, so I'll vote for Highgate being a separate place. The Halfway stood roofless for a while and is now a row of houses.

The towns had a discrete identity, coming under a Dearne Urban District Council until local government reorganisation in 1974[21], and turning partly towards Doncaster and partly towards Barnsley as far as entertainment and shopping went; to add to the mixture, the towns have a Rotherham telephone number.

An oddity, in terms of whether it leans towards Darfield and Wombwell or the Dearne towns, is the tiny village of Billingley, a place that was built round farming and, despite the presence of a tiny drift mine open for a few years in the 1950s, never became a pit village. In the Domesday Book it's recorded as a 'quite large' village and a stroll through it is a visceral reminder of the way that cultural and economic change can rip through even a tiny place like Billingley[22]. In the earlier years of the twentieth century there were two general stores, a butcher's shop, a slaughterhouse and a pub and even, in the 1920s, a fish and chip shop. These have all dried up, like the village pond, but the village hall has been restored with money from the Lottery and provides a centre for the place that perhaps the slaughterhouse never could.

Goldthorpe straddles the main road, or it did until the bypass sidestepped it. Like much of this part of the borough, it's an ancient settlement, with the name probably being a Viking one that means 'Golda's outlying farm', and it would have been a farming village for many hundreds of years until the discovery of coal. The landowner Lord Halifax, from his vantage point at Hickleton Hall, has been a big influence on the place. Halifax is an interesting figure, a major Conservative politician who held the post of Foreign Secretary before the Second World War and who could have been Prime Minister after Chamberlain's resignation. According to a local website, he would walk down the main street of Goldthorpe so that he could meet and greet the locals. That was good of him. I hope they doffed their caps and touched their forelocks.[23]

The Church of St John and St Mary is an astonishing building, even more astonishing for being in the middle of a pit village. It was commissioned by Lord Halifax in 1914 because of his new-found rich man's enthusiasm for concrete and his love of the Italian style. He got the architect Charles Young Nutt to design it and it is the first church building in the country to be made entirely of reinforced concrete and the only one in a former coalfield to look like it should be in a small Italian town. The tower housed four chimes that could be rung by clicking a switch and, as a former bellringer, I'm disappointed that they were removed in the 1950s.

The concrete that the church was made from reacted badly to the mucky South Yorkshire air and rain that played havoc with your washing if you left it out too long, and by the end of the last millennium it was in a crumbly state of repair. Luckily the Heritage Lottery stepped in, like they have with so many things round here, and helped to restore the church. In 2006 I was invited there, along with former local resident and professional shouter Brian Blessed, to an event to celebrate the commissioning of a new window in the church commemorating the men and boys who had died down the mines. Brian Blessed didn't arrive, and I made an inappropriate joke about the fact that he could just shout his words from whichever film set he happened to be on in America and that he wouldn't need a microphone and that anyway, if he had have turned up he'd have probably knocked the church down with the power of his gusty language. Even though it was three gags in one it still didn't get more than a dutiful murmur and a couple of moments of group pew-shuffling. Tough crowd.

There's a tiny convent in Goldthorpe, near the church, and for years as you passed through on the bus to Barnsley, you'd see nuns walking along the main street. I once saw one on a windy day, her habit blowing, juxtaposed with a slow-motion fight between two middle-aged men who had just trickled out of the taproom of the Waggon and Horses. A slow blow was landed and an antagonist's glasses fell to the floor. 'That's his glasses gone,' said a fellow passenger. 'I know his mam,' said another, which seemed unlikely, 'she'll be chuffin steamin!'

Because our visions of who we are and who we might become are settled in adolescence, I always associate Goldthorpe with wide skies and the Great American Road Trip; this is because, in 1970 I went to the Empire cinema in Goldthorpe with my mate Mark Smales to watch a double bill of *Midnight Cowboy* and *Easy Rider*, two films that have remained at the front of my cultural consciousness ever since. The cinema opened in 1910 when Goldthorpe was a boom town because of the local pits. Goldthorpe Colliery was opened the same year and Hickleton Main began work in 1892. Later, in 1912 Barnburgh Pit was opened, followed in 1916 by Highgate. The Empire closed in 1972 with the last picture show being that tissue-dampener *Love Story*[24]. Love means never having to say you're sorry, except to your mam when she asks about your shattered glasses. Because it was a gold rush kind of a settlement, although the gold was black, the town had more than one cinema, with the Picture House, built two years later next to Goldthorpe Hotel by the owner of the pub, Mr Whitaker. I'm always sorry that I never experienced Goldthorpe in its Klondyke days: it must have been quite a sight to see, with the nuns rushing through the rhythmic mayhem to mass, and Lord and Lady Halifax waving from a passing carriage and perhaps flicking coins.

In 1969, in an echo of Goldthorpe's barnstorming past, a man called Bill Kearns buried himself alive in the field opposite the Halfway pub that's now a housing estate. His plan was that he'd break the world self-incarceration record by keeping himself beneath the earth for 78 days and then when he came out of the ground like Ursula Andress emerging from the sea in *Dr No*, the people of the Dearne Valley would pay a tanner to watch his Lazarus-like rebirth. Sadly they didn't turn out in numbers and Bill lost £370.00 on the deal. Still, with true Yorkshire stoicism he said that he was proud he'd broken the record, and he's still remembered in Barnsley. Just. When we drove past the field around that time on our way through to Doncaster my dad would point and say 'He's still there!' and my mam would tell him not to be so daft and to keep his eyes on the road.

At the back of Goldthorpe's Central Business District there's a remarkable suite of buildings that represent a lost utopia of collectivism that is perhaps on its way to being restored to a certain, or rather an uncertain, extent. The buildings include the Town Hall, what was the Dearne Youth Club, the Cricket Club and yet another hidden gem of the Barnsley area, the Dearne Playhouse in what used to be Miners' Welfare Hall. To see all these buildings together in the same small geographical space is to imagine a place where the social, political, educational and cultural needs are met and nurtured and encouraged. Gaze and marvel.

Goldthorpe Station was opened in 1988, and my next port of call should be Thurnscoe, just a two minute ride up the line on the train from Leeds. I once got on the train there and a woman sat next to me with a plate of food under some kitchen foil. 'It's Sunday dinner. I'm taking it to my uncle in Bolton-on-Dearne,' she explained. 'My sister normally does it but she's gone to Cleethorpes.' I had to gently explain to her that she should have gone from the other platform on the Sheffield train. Still, Thurnscoe was only a short hop and then there was only about a half hour wait for the next train. I hope Uncle liked his Yorkshires cold.

Thurnscoe, like Goldthorpe, is an old settlement with layers of pit workings on top. It's situated on the old Roman road called Icknield Street, and was mentioned in the Domesday Book with a name that translates as Thorn Tree Wood. St Helen's Church is one of the oldest surviving buildings, and it's well worth a look. To stand for a moment or two in its churchyard and meditate is to be aware of all those who have stood on the site before. Roman soldiers, perhaps.

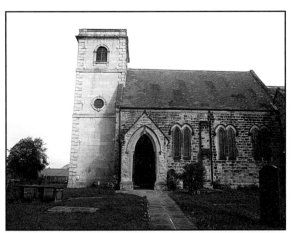

A woman remembering the time she got on the wrong train and the unchristian things the uncle said about the Yorkshire puddings that were like laminated menus by the time they arrived. Opposite the church is the lovely, simple building that is the Thurnscoe Little

Theatre, home of the Thurnscoe Amateur Dramatic Society and a beautiful small space that deserves to be more used.

The mining industry has certainly had a huge effect on Thurnscoe, both for its arrival and its departure. Much of the older housing in the village was built for the enormous Hickleton Main pit which at one time employed over 2000 men and which eventually closed in 1994. That same year, an ambitious community art project culminated in *Lullaby Tunnel*, an opera performed in the pit yard, commemorating the Barnburgh Pit disaster of 1942[25]. I remember being at a performance of the piece, with its fantastically challenging music by Karen Wimshurst and libretto by the Barnburgh-based playwright Ron Rose. Thousands of people saw the production over two days and I for one will never forget the sun going down behind the muckstack and the pithead gear as the final music lifted into the evening air. I recall that there was great hope expressed at the time for the site to be a permanent amphitheatre but the powers that be, whoever they are, had other ideas and the pithead gear was demolished and light industry sprang up all across where Hickleton Main used to be. It's well worth standing there and trying to remember how it was before, and thinking about how perhaps we'll remember the coal-mining industry as simply a moment or two in history's long game.

I could now recreate the journey of the woman with Uncle's dinner and get the train from Thurnscoe to Bolton on Dearne, the third of the Dearne towns triumvirate, unless you count (yeah, yeah) Highgate. Bolton on Dearne is called Bolton by locals and I always hope that somebody, hoping to get to Bolton, Lancs, ended up in this Bolton by mistake. I would say they were the winners, but of course I'm biased. Historically it was larger and more important than Goldthorpe or Thurnscoe and like those two villages it has a fascinating church that's well worth a look at. I think that, as lots of the big halls in this part of the world have been demolished or used for other purposes, the churches are the places where we can look for the tree-rings of history. The existing St Andrew's church is on a site that's been inhabited and used as a place of gathering and worship since before the Norman invasion in 1066. Inside, it's the usual history book in stone and glass: the Saxon window, the Norman window, the Jacobean pulpit. When so much of the past has been trampled on or rubbed out, churches can be living community centres that also double as museums. I know that the people who worship there would rather they weren't called anything to do with museums but they are gateways to a layered past that's in danger of being lost.

One of the great lost sites of Bolton on Dearne is the gun battery, situated just off Lowfield Road; it's all but forgotten now but it was a vital part of the local anti-aircraft defence in the Second World War after the Sheffield Blitz[26]. Over the years a number of groups have attempted to restore the site, which sits at the side of the Trans Pennine Trail, with varying degrees of success, but the ack-ack battery, as it's known locally, is one of only a two or three remaining in the country and was a significant local employer. The remains of a Nissen hut lead you to the concrete outbuildings and you get a sense of the scale and importance of the battery. Maybe the legacy of post-industrialisation is that these sites will still keep turning up in the front of peoples' minds, being dragged from the back of their minds by enthusiasts and volunteers who want to keep the memory of these places alive. On a tour of the Dearne towns (and Highgate, Yes, and Billingley, Yes) I have seen where a slaughterhouse was, where a little theatre is, where Brian Blessed walked the streets and where a nun's habit was darkened by afternoon rain.

JUNCTION 36

We're lucky in Barnsley because we've got two Motorway Junctions; three or two-and-a-half if you count Junction 38, which is more or less outside the borough. I'll come back to Junction 38 later, in a different section of the book. We're lucky because post-industrialisation could have abandoned us if our villages had been isolated and miles from main roads but they're not. Thank goodness (and I never thought I'd say this) for the M1.

Junction 36 is signposted Barnsley South and it takes you on to the A61 and the main road into Barnsley. It also joins up with a the bypass that rumbles, via a flock of roundabouts, down to the big and growing developments at Cortonwood and on to join the A635 and then the A1. My wife, daughter, grandson and I once drove down that bypass late on a foggy evening after visiting the theatre in Sheffield. Suddenly, as though in a subtitled film, four horses did what's known in the trade as a gloom-loom: they loomed through the gloom. We stopped. The horses had got loose from somewhere and I knew the damage they could do because a neighbour had recently had his car badly dented by a horse that leaped out on a bypass. The loose leaping gloom-loomers are the very worst. I rang the police. 'There are horses loose on the bypass near Junction 36,' I said, trying to sound calm and authoritative. 'What kind of horses?' the copper on the end of the line said. I tried to describe them as best I could. They were big, horse-shaped. 'Where exactly are they?' he asked.

This was when I became really, thunderingly aware that motorways and bypasses are like knives slicing through the landscape-cake. They may follow contours and existing bits of topography but they're also bullies, going where they want and shoving history out of the way. In other words, I wasn't really sure where I was. The fog didn't help either. 'Not far from the roundabout,' I stumbled along, conversationally; '…not the first roundabout but the second one. That's the one with the NMTF sign on it. Not far from Lowe Stand.' I realised I was speaking a kind of hyper-local gibberish. The horses had disappeared, which was a good thing. The motorway junction and the bypass were living in their own section of time and space, one that it was really hard to locate, and I've lived here all my life.

The first section of the M1 was opened in 1959 and the extension towards Yorkshire was built between 1965 and 1968, which is when Junction 36 was opened. For many years for the people of my side of Barnsley it was a kind of wayside halt of a junction, in my opinion, because from Darfield you had to go through Wombwell, Platts Common (there never was an apostrophe, self-styled saviours of grammar will be distressed to know) and Hoyland Common. Up the hill from Platts Common to Hoyland Common, when we used to go visiting my Uncle Jack and Auntie Mary in Hillsborough on Boxing Day, I always used to marvel at the house that had Christmas decorations strung across *the house* and all around the windows. I know this is commonplace these days but whoever had that house was a real pioneer. I used to ask my dad to slow down as we passed and he would always say 'He'll get a big bill in January', but I thought that was a price worth paying.

Now, though, since the Dearne Valley Parkway was built, we can zip to the motorway in twenty minutes and, more importantly in some ways, we can zip to the vast shopping kingdom that is Meadowhall, just down the motorway at Junction 34. In many ways Meadowhall is a good thing but there's no doubt it has sucked and continues to suck much of the life out of the town centres of Barnsley, Rotherham and Sheffield, another body blow that these places don't really need as they carry on their struggle with post-industrial reinvention.

Before writing this book I never thought very much about roads and how important they were; when I embarked on the writing of *Real Barnsley* I thought I might wax lyrical every now and then about old drovers' roads and cart tracks and pit lanes shaped by generations of boots. I didn't think I'd be crafting paragraphs about these new highways, but now I'm glad I am because they're important to the present and the future of the place I live in.

There's a tangle of businesses at Junction 36 and as I write this there's work going on to build new roundabouts that will ease the traffic flow in this particular morning and evening bottleneck. Right by the roundabout is the Rockingham Cricket Club's ground (named after Rockingham pit) where my grandson and his mates, when they're not bowling or batting for Darfield stand and gaze open-mouthed at the women doing Zumba dancing in the clubhouse. It's all part of growing up. I was the same with Pan's People.

The newest development at Junction 36 is a pub called the Dearne Valley Farm and a KFC. The name of the Dearne Valley Farm intrigues me: perhaps there was a farm there called the Dearne Valley but maybe there wasn't. Maybe the word 'farm' has more of a glow about it than the word 'bypass' and the pub is owned by a chain called Farmhouse Inns so maybe that's more of a clue, because all their pubs, whether in Wolverhampton or Paisley, are called something Farm. I like the fact that this part of the bypass is now a destination, that people can have a run out to the roundabout in the same way that our family used to have a run out to Brierley Crossroads to eat an ice cream. The flat-pack factories in the area don't have a lot of character. Maybe the Zumba dancers will go in for a pint after the class.

I do mourn the loss of the tiny bypass feral apple tree that used to sprout beautiful red apples each year. I never stopped to pick any but I told myself that one day I would and now I never will because the developers have ripped it away. I could probably have some apple juice in the Dearne Valley Farm but it won't be the same.

The Dearne Valley Parkway is the A6195 and it begins, in its present state, near Cat Hill in Darfield, at a roundabout that is called, oddly, Cathill, to sound like catheter. It rolls on past the Old Moor RSPB site[11], past an estate called Heron's Reach, and by the new development at Cortonwood, the site of one of the pits that started the miners' strike of 1984 when it was threatened with closure. There's a certain thudding postmodern irony about the fact that, in the café in the Cortonwood Morrisons, there are pictures of the pit. Still, any reminders of what was there before are good.

The bypass passes over a greened-over stretch of the old Wombwell canal and makes its way round the back of Wombwell, passing the Lundhill Tavern, then after more roundabouts that take you to Hemingfield and Jump and Platts Common and Hoyland Common, I would arrive at the motorway.

Just before the road was completed, in the early 90s, the poet and publisher Peter Mortimer walked along its emptiness as part of his *Broke Through Britain* odyssey, where he attempted, (and succeeded) to walk the length of the country without booking into any hotels or B&Bs and just relying on the kindness of strangers and the emergency tenner he had tucked into his sock. One of the rules he set himself for his quest was not to stay with anybody he knew but as he walked along the unopened road with aching feet and a sick dog he cracked and decided to come and stay at my house. Sadly I was on holiday at the time in Northumberland, not far from where Pete lives; luckily my neighbours, in the traditional Barnsley way, took him in, fed him and looked after his feet and his dog. I didn't envy Pete much of his jaunt but the bit that made me jealous was the idea of being the first on a road, the first to trudge along it before the cars roared past and the horses escaped. You would feel like Earl Fitzwilliam on the first barge down the new canal.

Much of Barnsley doesn't change much, but these motorway junctions do; they'll have changed since I wrote this. I reckon that if you want to chart the social, political and economic health of a region, particularly a region that's lost much of its traditional industry, then a motorway roundabout is well worth a visit.

WHERE WE WENT

I was born in 1956 in Darfield, the village where I still live, and in the 1960s I would hang around a lot with my mates and occasionally we would venture out of the village to, well, another village. Within the scope of *Real Barnsley* we would swing across South and sometimes into Central. Sometimes, by accident, we'd end up in North or West. Occasionally, by accident or design, we'd go to Sheffield but that is outside the scope of *Real Barnsley*.

It's interesting to note how self-contained these pit villages were. If you lived in Carlton you'd have no real need to go to Jump. If you lived in Thurnscoe why would you go to Cudworth? Everything you needed was in your little patch of ground and sky.

My wife reminds me that when she was at school and wanted to go from Darfield to Thurnscoe to visit her mate Lynsey in the mid-1970s she would write to her to ask if it was okay. Lynsey would write back and say yes and suggest a day and time. My wife would write and suggest a day and a time and Lynsey would write back and confirm it. She would then get on an LP Bus and travel the three miles to Thurnscoe, although the bus would take quite a while because it went via Middlecliffe, Great Houghton and Little Houghton, pausing for a while by Houghton Main pit so that Alvin the driver could nip out for a cigarette. By the time she got to Lynsey's house it was probably time to come back.

Me and the lads would wander around Darfield like people who couldn't find the house keys. We'd go up Barnsley Road and down Woodhall Road. We'd play on the fields that are now a big housing estate with so many Italian street names (Capri Court, Lombard Crescent) that some people call it the Italian Estate and some, with longer memories call it the Ideal Homes, after the long-defunct building firm who constructed them.

Every Saturday we'd get the bus to Wombwell even though, to be honest, we could have walked it. There's something of a rite of passage about catching a bus and also the fares in the Socialist Republic of South Yorkshire were so low at the time that the miniscule amount of shoe-leather used would probably have been more expensive than the trip on the upper deck.

In Wombwell we'd gravitate to a couple of shops. We'd have a look in Turvey's at the top of Station Lane; it was a kind of newsagent-plus and the more cerebral and geeky of us bought stamps for our collection. For some reason triangular ones were the most prized, as though they were coins you could spend on the market. We'd then wander down to the aforementioned market and congregate around the comic stall which was run by an irascible bloke who, every now and then, would point at a kid who was just hanging round the edge of the crowd and not buying any comics, and say, in a harsh and gratingly loud voice, 'I could do with losing ten per cent of my customers. Him for instance.' The child would melt away, and I would go cold hoping that he would never pick on me.

Sometimes we would then go to the Plaza Cinema for the Saturday matinée. It strikes me now that, in the mid-to-late 1960s, we were taking part in the dying throes of a long tradition stretching back decades. I recall a serial that felt old-fashioned and clunky even then, a series of short public information films and a main feature that you could never hear because people were whooping and screaming so much. In my head the main feature was in black and white but that can't be true, can it? One of my mates always took a spanner with him in case he got attacked by rough boys, presumably intent on stealing his triangular stamps from the French Territory of the Afars and Isars. I remember once a kind of floor show, a band of lads not much older than us who played guitars in a way that suggested their indulgent parents had bought them a lot of Shadows records from Neal's Music Shop in the arcade in Barnsley. The Plaza shut down as a cinema in 1967.

A Deep Tarn Calendar – January

If tha seez a snooerman
Wi a termater for a nooaz
An' eyes like bits er coyl
And wearing a deeead cap,

It int er snooerman
It's old Jack
Westerin' back from't club:
Tha can see eez singin'

Burriz words are frozz
When they leeeave his clack
And theer thi 'ang
Like ballooinz.

Melt 'em in front on't fire
Then tha car eear worree sed.
Listen to 'em
Sizzzzzzzle.

A Deep Tarn Calendar – February

Slairin darnt yard like a snowball rollin
Darn Snape Hill; ice as treacherous
As a knocker up that dint get
Knocked up. Left yer zizzin
And nar yer runnin
Ter catch up wi'February
That's comin rarnd bi't club
On a dubble decker o'Pepper's.

A Deep Tarn Calendar – March

Just
Just that
Just that bit
Just that bit leeter
On a morning.
Can tha see?
Like a reyt feeble
One bar electric fire
In a damp bedsit
Glowin under a dooor.

Notes

1. www.darfieldmuseum.co.uk My wife and I are normally there on the second Saturday of each month; however, if you visit on the first Saturday of the month you'll be able to get a bacon sarnie cooked by Hilary and Pauline, unless you're reading this many, many years in the future, or as you call it, The Present.
2. On the gatepost there's a sign that tells us the park was built in 1923 as a Miners' Welfare Park. There used to be a dog's grave in there and I've spent ages racking my brains and the internet but I can't find any photographs or the name of the dog.
3. There's still a road sign for Darfield Main Colliery as you drive out of Wombwell towards Barnsley. I guess it's pointing to history.
4. For years, after the pit had shut in 1993, you could still find evidence of the Women Against Pit Closures caravan that parked near the mine entrance. All that's gone now, too.
5. The Church Hall used to be the Empire Cinema, which closed in December 1956 after a final showing of *White Christmas*. I hope it was snowing.
6. You can see some of the coins at Darfield Museum. At least they're not still in Doncaster.
7. The Holiday cottage is called The Mistral. It's close to the Peak District apparently.
8. *Esther's Tomcat* by Ted Hughes covers the story poetically, and Sir Perceval Cresacre appears in *Ivanhoe* by Sir Walter Scott.
9. You can find this piece on the *Yorkshire Post* website www.yorkshirepost.co.uk where you can also find lots of articles about things mentioned in this book. They're mostly by me or Steve McLarence.
10. Iain Nicholls is on facebook and is well worth following. His paintings of Cat Hill capture its mystery.
11. Find Old Moor on the RSPB website. Perhaps go there when you're staying at The Mistral.
12. That's a joke, but not a bad one. You can use it if you want.
13. There's a Friends of West Haigh Wood because there are a considerable number of Enemies of West Haigh Wood who roar through it on bikes, churning it up.
14. Ebenezer Elliot's life and times are well worth exploring; his *Selected Poems* are available from Google Books, edited by Mark Storey.

15. You can find the account in the *The Star* from April 26th 2006.
16. Iain Nicholls's mother remembers it vividly.
17. There's an article about Albert Hirst in the first issue of *Old Barnsley* magazine from Autumn 2007.
18. For years I made little five minute programmes for Yorkshire Television to transmit at the end of their regional news. I went out and about finding odd stories and writing an instant poem which I would read from a reporter's notebook. YTV billed me as their Investigative Poet and my catchphrase was, turning back to the camera like Columbo: 'I'm just going for the Darfield Bus.' Nothing much changes.
19. The Friends of Wombwell Cemetery are very active and are always looking for new recruits. I guess it helps if you're local.
20. One of the bands I saw at the Halfway was the 1970s band Burlesque which counted as one of its members the blues guitarist Billy Jenkins. I did a gig with him years later and told him about it and he said that he remembered me standing by the speakers and he said to his fellow band members that one day we'd work together. I really wanted to believe him.
21. The Urban District Councils were abolished in 1974; many of the local minutes are kept in the Barnsley Archives and I would love to have the time to read them all.
22. You can find lots about Billingley on the local website www.billingleyvillage.co.uk
23. There used to be a plaque on the village green at Hickleton that said THE EARL OF HALIFAX INVITES YOU TO REST AWHILE AND ENJOY HICKLETON
24. The Cinematreasures.org website is, as some people say, a mine of information for this kind of thing.
25. I've heard odd recordings of bits of *Lullaby Tunnel* and I really would love to see it revived. Any takers?
26. Some fantastic pictures of the gun battery on exploringtheunderbelly.wordpress.com

CENTRAL

ARDSLEY

You can gauge the popularity of Barnsley F.C. by how busy it gets down Ardsley Hill to Stairfoot Roundabout; during our long-distant season in the Premiership (I mean our first season in the Premiership, of course) traffic backed up towards the Crematorium and sometimes back towards the Yew Tree Garden Centre; in the dark days of League One struggle you could slip straight down the hill like an ambulance on the way to the hospital. One night, when we played and beat Spurs in the FA Cup and the traffic was almost back to my house in Darfield, a Spurs fan leaned out of his car to ask for directions. I resisted the temptation to send him the wrong way, like a Tranmere fan once did to me when I was stewarding Bus 3, and pointed him in the right direction through the traffic jam. 'Is it always this quiet round here?' he asked, teaching me a lesson about the differences between life in a city and life in a small town. I grinned. I noticed that he had a model of the FA Cup made out of silver foil in the back of his car. This may have been the same one I saw in a gutter near Oakwell the next day.

For those of us on this side of town, Ardsley is defined by the hill, by the way it straddles the A635, which is a shame because if you stop and look, there's more to Ardsley than that. In the churchyard of Christ Church there's a memorial to commemorate the dead of the explosion at the nearby Oaks Colliery in 1866; the monument was recently cleaned up for the 150th anniversary of the explosion, and forms the centrepiece of a proposed Oaks Trail that will take you around the forgotten and faded landmarks. Christ Church was built in 1841 and it's worth looking inside at the sombre and moving memorials to the fallen of the First World War.

Walking past the church and up the hill out of town you come to the site of the former Ardsley House Hotel which was at one time Barnsley's only posh hotel. As a callow youth courting the girl who became my wife I took her to the Ardsley House for a meal. I dripped perspiration and sophistication when I ordered a half-bottle of Mateus Rose and swilled it round my mouth as the waiter looked on with a face like the front of a DAF truck. I pronounced it satisfactory and dribbled a bit down the tie that matched my shirt.

The name Ardsley comes from the Saxon word 'leah', meaning a clearing in a forest, and the name 'Eored', so Ardsley is Eored's

Clearing in a Forest which chimes in with other local names like Hunningley which would have been Hund's Forest Clearing. Sitting on the X19 on the way to Barnsley (upstairs at the front, of course, pretending to drive) you could be forgiven for forgetting that once this area was covered with the vast forest known as the Wildwood and that all we've done since then is carve out a bit of space for ourselves.

As I explain later (page 82), there's a lot of bad feeling towards Stairfoot Roundabout, which funnels traffic up and down the hill to and from Ardsley; a lot of this is due to the perception (and I can't comment on this because I can't drive) that, as my wife says 'They've got the lights on a funny setting' but there's a lingering sense of distaste at the way the roundabout was built across and on top of several sights of great archaeological and historical significance, following on from earlier 'flatten-it' thinking when the trains came. Hard to picture it now, but at one time there was almost a separate village set around a village just below the site of the existing Ardsley Oaks School, with a village green and a blacksmith's shop, which was destroyed when the railway arrived in the nineteenth century, and then older farm buildings were reputed to have been put under the tarmac when the roundabout was built. They've got that history on a funny setting, you know.

After being a quiet agricultural settlement for many years Ardsley began to grow, along with the rest of Barnsley, with the coming of the industrial revolution and the building of the Dearne and Dove Canal between 1793 and 1804. The equivalent of the Barnsley F.C. queue of traffic began to happen as tanning and weaving and the bleaching of linen took place on, yes, an industrial scale. When the South Yorkshire Railway arrived in 1841 the population grew hugely along with shops, churches and schools. Gas, I'm reliably informed, arrived in Ardsley in 1871, presumably by barge. I'm not a historian, I'm a poet. Sadly, a dry archaeological report, *The Ardsley House Archaeological Assessment*, states, with almost an official lump in its throat and occasional tortured syntax, 'Most of the Historic buildings of Ardsley, some dating back to the medieval period, and many 200 years or later [sic], were demolished without record in the late 1950s and early 1960s. In addition, several historic street names were lost with the creation of the new dual carriageway, which had previously encompassed several road names, which was wholly renamed Doncaster Road.' This explains why my mate Tony lives at number six hundred and seventy odd.

The Ardsley House, which is in the process of being demolished as I write this, was a fine manor house built in the late 1770s by the Micklethwait family who continued to live in it until the last Squire of Ardsley, Richard Gerald Micklethwait left just after the Second World War. It's an odd thought to me that the Socialist Republic of South Yorkshire had squires and gentry until comparatively late in the twentieth century, but maybe it shouldn't surprise me because these were the landowners who helped, by fair means or foul, the rapid progress of industrialisation that completely transformed these fields and hamlets. There was a steep area behind Ardsley House called the Cheese Fall, and I like to imagine Micklethwait and his waistcoated mates rolling cheeses down it for local lads to chase with the promise of a gill of beer afterwards. Only the promise, of course. They didn't actually give any out. How did you think they afforded those natty waistcoats?

The house was leased to the National Coal Board in 1960, which is why some older people in Ardsley still refer to it as 'the pit offices' and then it became the hotel where I ordered my half bottle of Mateus in 1972. It's sad to see it go and it seems to me that much of the history of Ardsley has simply been screwed up and chucked into a bin.

At the back of the house is the Crematorium, a place of almost overwhelming melancholy and functionality. There's a kind of peace there, but a kind of floating peace, unlike the earthier peace of a churchyard.

Walk down towards Darfield from Ardsley and I pass a number of feral apple trees. One day, in a ghost version of this book, I'll write about all the wayside apple trees you can find round here, grown from cores (or cokes as one local variation has it) flung from car windows by passing motorists. What I like about feral apple trees is that they're examples of survival against all the odds. So many apples flung; so few trees grown. If you see a man in late-middle age scrambling up a bank of earth by the side of the main road, clutching an Aldi carrier bag and grinning widely, you know I've just found some proto-pies and crumbles. I often wish there was a better name for them than 'feral'; I'm sure I'll come up with something on my wanderings. Wild? Gift? Unregarded? Hardcore?

Living in the same place all your life (so far) you think you know it like the back of your hand, and yet one day a number of years ago I turned down a track off the A635, alerted by a For Sale sign and came across a big house that you can't visit because it's private and protected but it's still intriguing to me that it exists. It's called Cranford Hall or New Hall and it's often described in estate agents' speak as 'a Victorian gentleman's residence' although there's evidence that there was a medieval hall on the site. It's another example of the hidden history of this part of the world, feral apples of the sun, as W.B. Yeats more or less said.

At the other side of Stairfoot Roundabout from Ardsley towards Barnsley, you'll pass the part of Barnsley known as Kendray. One very unusual thing about Kendray is that there are very few 'ay' endings in English place names. I can only think of Bungay in Suffolk. When TV producers or journalists come to talk to me and want to film or photograph me by a 'typical Barnsley view' I don't take them down to Barnsley Main, our one remaining pithead. Remarkable and majestic though it is, I take them up to

the top of Kendray where they can look out at the town laid out like an architect's drawing. Kendray is mainly a huge postwar housing estate that has undergone extensive renovation; the local wild area is known as The Swanee, and Kendrayers will tell you tales of running through it and swimming in it and catching tadpoles in it.

By the side of Doncaster Road, opposite the memorial to the rescuers who were involved in the explosions at the Oaks Colliery, you'll find Kendray Hospital, a suite of buildings that's got a long history, starting life as a fever hospital in 1890, which then became a place for geriatric patients, and has latterly been used for people with mental health problems. I once visited there to give a talk; a man stopped me in the corridor and said 'Are you the turn?'. I said that I was. He looked me in the eye and spoke in a hoarse whisper, a bit like Private Fraser in *Dad's Army*. 'Well, just one thing: I hope you're funnier than that Laughter Therapist we had that time.' So did I. Halfway through my turn I caught his eye and he raised a thumb. Result! I'm funnier than a laughter therapist. That'll be going on my CV.

The railway line between Leeds or Huddersfield and Sheffield runs through Kendray, and as you wait in the traffic to go up Kendray Hill towards town you can see the ancient trains rattling by and it's always struck me as odd that it hasn't got a station. Mind you, if I said that, some people round here they'd look at me like I was a laughter therapist.

And now I'm back at Stairfoot Roundabout, the whirlpool that snags all of Barnsley in its maelstrom. On the right, near where the Aldi is, the Hope Glass Works were built in the 1870s and it was there that Ben Rylands perfected the manufacturing process for the Codd bottle developed by the wonderfully-named Hiram Codd.

Think of the trains thundering through here; think of the clink of the Codd bottles and the stink of the bleached linen drying on the fields. Think of the sound of the long-demolished blacksmith's shop and think of the sound of feral apples falling to the floor. Layers of history, making you smile. A kind of laughter therapy all on its own. What's that word? Palimpsest.

THE OAKS DISASTER

Because Barnsley is built around, and on top of, and in the wake of, coal mining, much of the life of the borough is lived in the shadow of death's visible and invisible symbols, the memorials and commemorative plates and broadsheets that are the street furniture and household gods of industrialisation. You could do a kind of macabre but faintly comforting (because you're sure it won't happen again) walk around the plaques and obelisks that dot-to-dot the map, taking in grassy knolls and deserted bus shelters and the surviving headgear of Barnsley Main.

There were large and small pit disasters all across the town and the surrounding villages; the Swaithe Main disaster, the site of which can be reached from a path round the back of the empty B&Q, killed 143 miners in December 1875, and a sombre, subtle memorial stands in the churchyard at Worsbrough. In Darfield, the Friends of Darfield Churchyard (we'll all be friends of the churchyard in the end, I know) restored the beautiful Lundhill Colliery Disaster Memorial, a pale and imposing monument that stands over the River Dearne's twisting curves. Lundhill Colliery was situated between Wombwell and Elsecar, on a site that's now a golf course and not too far from the Lundhill Tavern where I once got locked in with tight beer-locks in the company of a number of local head teachers after we lost the quiz by several points.

A steady walk up from Wombwell town centre brings me to a place that feels too peaceful to have been the site of all this carnage, but that's the thing about the post-coal landscape; it will never return to the pastoral setting that it was before they found the black diamonds, but somehow there's a species of uneasy peace, as though somebody has just popped out to the shop and left the broken door hanging on its hinges.

The Lundhill disaster happened in February 1857 and 189 men were killed in an explosion, a huge number but sadly dwarfed by the Oaks explosions that happened nine years later. Away from the vast massacres the tiny accidents, crushings and roof-falls still leave their marks. Quite literally, on the hands and legs of the men who survive, and psychologically on communities that relied on the men working under their feet to come home safely so that years, generations, later their sisters and sons could lose at a music quiz. The Houghton Main explosion happened in June 1975; five men from Darfield and the surrounding villages died, and I remember people standing around street corners waiting for the pit bus to arrive. The news rushed through back yards as though blown by a terrible breeze; odd to think of it now, but very few people had telephones and not all that many had cars. I recall thinking at the time, as the girlfriend who is now my wife waited for her dad to come home from Houghton Main, that the scenes were like something from the 1930s. I may even, in my pretentious teenage way, have called them Lawrentian. I really hope I didn't.

The Oaks was the enormous disaster that still rings like a muffled bell round these parts. At an event to mark the 150th anniversary at Barnsley Town Hall a dapper man who looked a bit like Captain Mainwearing came up to me and told me he was the great grandson of one of the rescuers; his three piece suit shone in the striplights and I wanted to talk to him about his great grandad's exploits but he soon melted into the crowd, seemingly happy that he'd brought his ancestor into the room.

The disaster happened on the morning of December 12th 1866 when the first of two explosions ripped through the pit. The final count of the dead is ambiguous and argued over; some sources say 361 men and boys (always that melancholy clause, always the men and the boys) some put the toll in the 380s. Like many disaster sites, the actual place of the horror is covered by a layer of unfeeling banality. You could play golf not far from the Lundhill disaster, and traffic rumbles over the burial ground of the Oaks disaster as people drive to the Tesco superstore at Stairfoot.

I start my Oaks memorial walk at the churchyard of Christ Church, Ardsley, where a memorial to some of the victims was erected by public subscription in 1879. It's a small, austere and thoughtful obelisk, mentioning (those shifting numbers again) 354 victims, 35 of whom are buried in the churchyard. Up the hill from the church is Ardsley House, which for many years was the area's only posh hotel which as I write is closed and awaiting conversion to flats.

From Ardsley Church I walk down past the brickworks and onto the old railway line that's now part of the Trans Pennine Trail. You could walk from here to Liverpool or Hull, mostly on these disused trackbeds, although that would be a hell of a weekend, from one City of Culture to another, and we'll stumble onto the TPT (as those in the know call it) elsewhere in the book. I turn right towards where the site of the Oaks pit was; I pass what used to be the Fossil Bank, a minor geological sensation that was part of the fabric of my kids' lives in the late 1980s. It was (and still is, although it's much less visible) an outcrop of rock from a time when Barnsley was part of a steaming tropical jungle and local head-teacher and artist Tony Heald recognised its educational and cultural potential and persuaded his mate at the brickworks to put a fingerpost up directing people to the Fossil Bank.

Me and my wife and kids spent many happy Sunday afternoons there with my mam's old magnifying glass and a brace of tiny trowels and a see-through bag to keep the fossils in. Sometimes we found small shards of pre-history and sometimes we just pretended we had, like when I screeched to the lads that I'd seen Stephenson's Rocket in the distance on a train-spotting trip to the pit yard. 'Don't get too excited,' I'd say, holding up what could have been a cardigan button, 'but I think I've found part of the tooth of a triceratops'. They'd all clamour around me and I'd hold it up in the air like I was raising the flag at Iwo Jima and I'd almost believe it myself.

I cross the road at Stairfoot Roundabout, an odd black hole of radio reception-lack, where you have to lean in and try to filter the muttering hiss to catch some grumbling or praising on *Praise or Grumble*, the venerable BBC Radio Sheffield phone-in on your way back from Oakwell, and I walk down a nondescript track that has carrier bags hanging from the trees and McDonald's detritus threatening to take over.

I went on a guided walk about the Oaks disaster once and the guide stopped us here, in this non-place. I thought he'd seen a 20p piece shining by the chip forks. 'Below here is where the accident happened,' he said, and I felt a chill.

After the first explosion which ripped through the workings a number of rescuers bravely went down into the pit to try and get survivors and bodies out. They found dead and injured miners in, to quote a contemporary source, 'various conditions of ghastliness' which conjures up images that keep me awake at night, and the rescue work continued for the rest of the day. The wonderfully-named mine engineer Parkin Jeffcock went down into the smoky hell and was concerned that the pit was heating up again and he was right to be concerned as a second explosion thundered through the tight spaces of the shaft and the tunnels, killing most of those below ground. There was a third explosion, and a fourth, and more and more, like blows raining on a slumped and defeated boxer.

I stand and look around. Maybe somehow, somewhere, the echoes of these explosions still lingers minutely, cupped in a fallen leaf or sticking to a tree root.

I turn and walk towards Kendray Hill and the spectacular statue erected to commemorate the rescuers. Before the widespread commemorations of the 150th anniversary of the disaster in 2016, the accepted wisdom was that this representation of an angel clutching a fallen hero was a memorial to the disaster itself, but that isn't the case. In 1913 by local philanthropist and art lover Samuel Cooper (of the eponymous Cooper Gallery) decided it should be put up and, so the story goes, just happened to have a statue in his back garden. That's philanthropy for you.

THE ALHAMBRA AND SHEFFIELD ROAD

Over the years in Barnsley, 'meet you at the Alhambra' has morphed its meaning so that it now means something completely different to what it did half a century ago.

Older people in the town still remember the Alhambra; it was opened in 1915 by (surprise) Countess Fitzwilliam from Wentworth Woodhouse and was a huge theatre space with more than two and a half thousand seats on four levels, including, amazingly, stalls and three balconies. It carried on as a live theatre for ten years but then, in common with many other performance spaces, it was converted into a cinema which flourished for many years but closed in 1960 with Laurence Olivier's *The Entertainer* sending the folks of the town out into the harsh November night. It reopened as a bingo club and stayed as a palace of the dabber pen until 1979. I can remember the plans around at the time to reopen the building as a repertory theatre, but it was eventually demolished in 1982 to make way for a new shopping centre, also called the Alhambra, which is of course what people younger than me mean when they arrange to meet there.

Getting off the bus on Sheffield Road you walk beneath an underpass and by a metal sculpture called 'The Alhambra Cat', reflecting the tales of theatre cats who prowled around the stalls and backstage when the audience had gone home. You can sit on a bench and gaze around but it's very difficult (and believe me, I've tried) to imagine the old Alhambra. I stand up and walk into the Alhambra Shopping Centre and buy a memory stick but I don't have any memories to stick in it.

I quite like the Alhambra Shopping Centre; these days it's called The Mall but I can't bring myself to call it that because malls are what you find in places like Delaware or South Dakota rather than Barnsley. It's been open since 1991 and we've grown used to it; you can often see people standing there having what Barnsley people call a 'kall', which is a beautifully resonant word meaning 'gossip' and 'chat'. It's a useful place to linger in on your way into the main shopping street in town and statistics tell us that people typically spend 25 minutes there. Well, I probably spend a little less time but then I'm often keen to get to the market.

Barnsley town centre is undergoing huge transformation as I write this and as you read it most of it will probably have been completed. We denizens (I think I'd rather be a denizen than a citizen: it's a more resonant word) of Barnsley are used to the idea of the town being remade and rebuilt and indeed there have been ambitious plans to remake the place since the pits shut. I'm an incurable optimist so I am convinced that this latest unfolding of the architects' maps will really work: there will be a new library as the centrepiece of a boulevard down which people like me and my wife and our children and grandchildren will walk like figures on one of the aforementioned architects' plans.

Moving out of Barnsley in the other direction, along Sheffield Road, I pass an area of smaller shops and takeaways and some older buildings and will then make my way up Mount Vernon Road towards Mount Vernon Hospital. I stroll by the old fountain and horse trough by the side of the road. The fountain was given as a gift to the town by the Reverend John Mason in 1888, on Coronation Day and I like the fact that the *Barnsley Chronicle* report from the time gives the exact details of the size and dimensions of the fountain and trough ('8ft in height with granite bowl 3ft 4in and a cattle trough measuring 6ft 3in) and then, with an in-print version of a Parisian shrug, says 'Under the cattle trough is a lesser one for the use of dogs etc.', leading me to wonder what the etceteras were and if they included ferrets, and I really hope they did.

After speeches and a rendition of 'God Save the Queen', the fountain was declared open. I felt ever so slightly jealous when I read about this because I've opened many things in my time, but never a fountain. I once opened a school library and as I did so a man in a hi-vis jacket came in and handed me a box of books to sign for what some present thought was a premeditated event. In one year I opened two sewage works and led school pupils around them and then made poems that were fresh and pure. I once opened a new community centre in Barnsley and they thought it was a good idea for me to stand on a set of fire escape steps and recite my poem of opening standing next to an extractor fan that sounded like Japanese noise music. My mouth opened and shut and opened and shut and I snipped a ribbon and it was as though the community centre had been opened by Marcel Marceau.

After the Sheffield Road fountain was declared open, the first glass of water was glugged by Mrs Mason and the second by the Reverend Mason, who then proceeded, in an act of Christian charity, to give out glasses of cool water to passers-by. Maybe I should have done the same at the sewage works. I have a fantasy that when the official party had gone, a shy man approached and allowed his stoat to drink from the lesser trough.

Stand by the fountain and the trough and meditate on the idea of free water for all, perhaps in the rain, and then you can make your way up to what began life as Mount Vernon Sanatorium which was acquired by Barnsley and Wakefield Councils in 1915 for use as a TB hospital. It was originally a house owned by those Barnsley bastions and patrons of the arts Samuel and Fanny Cooper: the names of just a few families wash over this town in all kinds of ways. I guess that's true of every small town but it seems really pervasive in Barnsley. Part of me worries away at a fantasy of what the borough would have been like if the Coopers and the Fitzwilliams and the Spencer Stanhopes hadn't been around. This would have been a very different place, that's for sure. Maybe the McMillans would have had to step in. Mount Vernon was a sanatorium until 1949, when it became Mount Vernon Hospital; expansion happened in the 1960s and 1970s when patients were transferred from Kendray and Lundwood hospitals. Lundwood was a hospital that I knew very little about before I started writing this book: it was originally a smallpox hospital from the turn of the twentieth century up until the founding of the NHS; after 1948 it became a hospital for older patients or as they called them in those far-off times, a geriatric hospital. In February 1977 Lundwood Hospital was burned and damaged, it was said to get rid of the old smallpox bugs, but also, perhaps, to exorcise the resident ghosts.

If you can have fond memories of a hospital, then I have to say that I have fond memories of Mount Vernon Hospital because the staff there worked extraordinarily hard to rehabilitate both of my parents after their respective illnesses. I remember long Sunday afternoons listening to them and encouraging them as they learned to talk and walk, and taking our children to the tiny and welcoming hospital shop that always felt like something from an H.G. Wells short story.

I guess a relationship with a town's hospitals is something that a visitor rarely has, and then only superficially. You come to the Cooper Gallery for the day from the Midlands and trip over your shoelaces and end up in Barnsley Hospital for a couple of hours and then you go home. That's one kind of experience, not to compare with my memories of my three children being born in Barnsley Hospital, or the care my parents got in there or in Kendray or in Mount Vernon. Memory is a tin of paint that you can't help dripping all over the places you walk through, and the longer you live somewhere the more the tin drips.

THE CULTURAL QUARTER

Here I am standing outside Barnsley's magnificent jewel of a Town Hall, ready for a stroll through what I'm going to insist on calling the Cultural Quarter, because that's what it is. I insist. Think of this section of the book as a cultural experience; imagine me as an audio guide whispering in your ear, or a one-man show at a fringe festival. Have you got your headphones in? I don't need them back; you can keep them as a souvenir.

The Town Hall, is a gleaming geometric and imposing Portland Stone edifice designed by the Liverpool-based architect Arnold Thornely, who also gave us the delights of the Stormont Parliament and other town halls in Wallasey and Preston. It was opened in December 1933 by the Prince of Wales who was then, no doubt, introduced to the delights of the Barnsley Chop, a cultural quarter on a plate. For those outside this particular culinary loop, a Barnsley Chop is most of a lamb almost drowned in a tide of gravy. It's officially a double loin chop with a little underfillet but unofficially it's a reyt gobfull. I like the Town Hall because, like many other town halls all over the country, indeed all over the world, it's a concrete (Portland Stone) symbol of civic pride, announcing that here is a place worth reckoning with.

Many town halls in these crushed-by-Toff times are undergoing transformations into hotels or apartments, but Barnsley, in a fleet-of-foot and quick thinking initiative, turned much of the floor space of the Town Hall into a museum of peoples' history, Experience Barnsley. The museum opened in 2013 and has been a huge and unfolding and growing success because it reflects the culture of Barnsley back to itself, giving us Albert Hurst's Pork Pie memorabilia alongside photographs of Charlie Williams and interactive mines for the kiddies to venture into. Let me declare an interest here: I'm on the Board of Trustees of Barnsley Museums and Heritage and so anything I say should be taken with a pinch of glee. I know that many other local authorities have cut down on museums and closed some of them but here in Barnsley the sector is thriving. Is it because I'm on the Board of Trustees (that's me in the corner of the meeting, eating a biscuit)? I couldn't possibly say. More biscuits?

Outside the Town Hall, by the War Memorial, is a sculpture borrowed from the Yorkshire Sculpture Park; it's called 'Crossing (Vertical)', by Nigel Hall, and it's a rusting abstract that challenges you think about the difference between the indoors and the outdoors, and I love it. I think it defines the space beautifully as people gambol in a Barnsley fashion (ie: keeping their caps on) in the timed fountains. The piece divides opinion though, it's fair to say, with local songwriter and cultural activist Dave Cherry calling it a 'nit comb' last time I saw him. Isn't that the great thing about art, though? One man's nit comb is another man's 'Crossing

(Vertical)'. Indeed, 'Crossing (Vertical)' forms one axis of a nascent Barnsley Sculpture Park because at the other side of the Town Hall, a little way up the hill towards Huddersfield Road, is local but internationally renowned sculptor Graham Ibbeson's wonderful representation of Barnsley's Greatest Cricket Umpire, Harold 'Dickie' Bird, finger eternally raised to the sky to give somebody out, presumably LBW.

Sadly, over the years since the piece was first plinthed, the cricketing finger has been used as a Saturday night hanger for a range of lingerie, thongs and knickers flapping in the breeze. Indeed, when I made a little TV film about the town a few years ago I was persuaded, although I didn't take much persuading, to buy some huge curtain-sized pants from a stall on the market to wrap around the digit. Letters of pant-protest were written to the *Barnsley Chronicle*, although I'm sure it made Dickie laugh. Mind you, he did persuade Graham Ibbeson to raise the plinth, but that only made the underwear tricksters more adventurous and, I guess (have you thought about this, Dickie?) more prone to injury and insurance claims.

I enjoy standing and marvelling at the Town Hall, though, before venturing into the Cultural Quarter; gaze up at the balcony where, in 2016, Paul Heckingbottom and the glorious Barnsley F.C. team paraded the League One winners trophy in front of an adoring

Barnsley crowd after our unprecedented second visit to Wembley in one wonderful season.

> Tell yer mam, yer mam
> To put the champagne on ice
> We're going to Wembley twice
> Tell yer mam, yer mam!

As the song went. All small towns should have moments like these, and sport can often provide them; arts can too, but that's a slower burn.

Now cross the road and walk up the hill a little to the Cooper Gallery. The building that's now the gallery was built in 1769 as the town's Grammar School and was later bought by local philanthropist and art-lover Samuel Joshua Cooper to create a gallery for the whole of Barnsley to enjoy, and it opened to the public in 1914. After being commandeered as an annexe of the hospital in the Second World War, it became a gallery again in 1957 and has been the beating artistic heart of the town ever since. For many years as a younger man I ran regular schools workshops there in the company of the genial but taciturn curator Don. I never knew his second name. Maybe he never knew mine.

When the schools came we always offered the teachers and assistants a cup of tea; Don would write down the orders on the back of an invitation to a long-forgotten retrospective and disappear into the kitchen upstairs to manhandle and cajole the World's Oldest Kettle which was rumoured to have belonged to Cooper himself.

Then he'd bring the tea downstairs on a tray that never seemed quite fit for purpose and one day wasn't. It collapsed more or less at the same time as Don tripped and the tea and the council milk jug performed circus tricks all over his suit as the tray clattered down the stairs. A large number of people tried not to laugh, a few succeeding, and Don stoically returned to the kitchen to make more drinks. This was in the long-lost time before internet memes and viral hits but I reckon that these days the Collapsing Don would have been an internet meme and a viral hit.

It was often the case that when the school parties came there would be an exhibition that involved some depiction of nudity and my job was to stand in front of the offending piece of art and direct kids to the innocent pictures on the other walls. It sometimes worked. It often didn't. Sometimes the adult art was three-dimensional and would jab me in the back, another internet meme before its time.

I always like to take my time around the Cooper Gallery; there will be a temporary exhibition on, and also, in the new extension at the back, an exhibition of the art collectors who have donated work to the gallery over the years for reasons of philanthropy or vanity or a combination of the two. I'm a chap who likes to slow the clock right down around a gallery, a chap who likes to stand in front of a painting for so long that the assistants think I've died and the public think I'm a conceptual piece called 'Crossing (Horizontal)'. The longer you look, the more you see, as the saying goes; I never see the point of scuttling round a gallery like you're on a supermARTet sweep.

Exit the Cooper Gallery and walk down the hill towards the town centre and then turn left to The Civic, the reconstruction of Barnsley's Old Civic Hall, which opened in 2009. The Civic Hall was a vast barn of a space that nevertheless edged its way into the heart of the town. It was seeing Bob and Carole Pegg's band Mr Fox there in 1972 that convinced me and the lads that our nascent pop group, Oscar the Frog, should take a lurch into folk/rock; at the pantomime when my kids were little a comedian stepped forward and asked the thin crowd 'How's Barnsley gone on?' which set up a slow middle-aged fist-fight in the stalls. When my wife and I were first courting, as they say round here, our Saturday night cutting-edge destination was a visit to the Folk Club in the upstairs Centenary Rooms. It wasn't quite Greenwich Village but we pretended that it was, and sometimes we even sang along with the choruses.

In an awful echo of the many mining disasters that have blighted the area, there was a disaster in January 1908 as the then public hall hosted a moving picture show for local children. There was a crush when some of the young people tried to get downstairs for a better view and sadly sixteen died and forty were injured. Wander down to the Civic and then wander up (lots of wandering in this part of town, or strolling, or trudging) the stairs and take a look in the massive gallery there. The Civic is an interesting experiment, putting on comedy, music and a lot of non-mainstream theatre; trying to build up an audience for the work isn't easy but I reckon it's extremely worthwhile and I'd urge anybody in town to visit the Civic.

Now that I've whetted your theatrical appetite, I'll stroll (or wander, if you like) back to the other end of the town's cultural quarter and have a look at the Lamproom Theatre. I don't normally like to use phrases like 'hidden gem' but I really do think it's a Hidden Gem. Dwarfed by offices, a Premier Inn and the Gateway Plaza apartment block, the Lamproom presents local amateur and professional groups and has built up a reputation for presenting, like the best community art does, the town back to itself culturally.

The building is an old Methodist chapel which was converted by a group of enthusiasts and opened in 1999; for a performer or an audience member it's a delightfully intimate space and it's an integral part of the theatrical ecology of the town. As an audience member there I know that I have to remain bright and alert because this conveys itself straight to the performers; any yawn, stifled or not, would dishearten anybody making their way through an Alan Ayckbourn play that relied on total and absolute concentration. You should always be a good audience member, of course, but at tiny and therefore more exciting venues like the Lamproom be continually alert.

One of the great things about the Cultural Quarter in Barnsley is that you can now get a good, imaginative and sharp espresso in one or all of the cafés at the venues. Years ago the town was an espresso desert. As a young sophisticate trying to impress my wife (we'd moved on from the folk club) I would march into cafés and order an espresso and the people behind the counter might assume I was asking for a bag of exotically flavoured crisps. Then when the espresso did arrive, in the 1990s at the Aroma Café in The Arcade, people were often astonished that I wanted to pay good money for something so small. 'Tha only gets a gobfull of pissing Maxwell House' as I once heard a man say, trying to describe the holiday espresso experience to his disbelieving mate. 'You do realise that's a small black coffee,' the person behind the counter would say, and I would give a worldly nod and say 'Oh yes. Make it a double' which might confuse them even more. These days the espressos flow. Well, they drip.

OAKWELL

I walk along Doncaster Road in Barnsley and I pass the site of the old Slazenger's tennis ball factory where I was gainfully employed in the 1980s putting glue on tennis balls then sticking them together; the factory has gone now and has been replaced by an estate of houses called Tuscany Gardens after the architect Will Alsop, in the early years of this century, said that Barnsley could be The New Tuscany. I remember appearing in the Richard and Judy studio to talk about it, while on location in the middle of town in the middle of a gale, the Mayor of Barnsley and Dickie Bird tried to recreate a bit of café society as ungainly umbrellas flapped.

I take a little detour into Barnsley Cemetery, opened in 1861 as a municipal burial place and still in use. It's a broad acre of the departed, with the graves of some of the dead from the Oaks disaster alongside many final resting places of linen and coal bosses. The gatehouses are now private dwellings, and as somebody who's lived behind a cemetery for decades, there's something comforting and oddly life enhancing about sharing space with those who have passed away.

I amble a little further up Doncaster Road to St Peter's Church, a redbrick building that was the parish church of the Reverend Tiverton Preedy, the enlightened muscular Christian who set up Barnsley Football Club in 1887, four digits that lots of Barnsley fans have as the pin number for their bank accounts, but don't tell anybody I told you. St Peter's was called a 'hidden gem' by Sir John Betjeman and it really is the most gorgeous building in the Anglo-Catholic tradition, and well worth a visit away from the Doncaster Road bustle. Inside the present church, which was opened for worship in 1911, the high altar was designed by Robert Thompson, the Mouseman of Kilburn who carved a mouse into his designs, and the whole church was designed by the renowned church architect Temple Moore, and is, I'm told, typical of the kind of work he created.

Tiverton Preedy, so the story goes, overheard some local men talking about setting up a football team and decided to take the project on, reasoning that it would keep them off the streets. He was influential in buying the land on which Barnsley F.C. still stands and the club has so much to thank him for, exemplified by a group of fans who made the pilgrimage to his grave in London in 2016 to tidy it up and lay flowers.

I turn right from the church and walk down to Oakwell, the home of the mighty, mighty, Barnsley F.C.. Ok, I'm biased. I've been a fan for twenty-odd years, brought to the team by my children, which is the opposite of what normally happens, I realise. My dad was more of a fisherman than a football fan, although he did occasionally hanker after his old team, Third Lanark, so I was never taken to the football as a boy. My kids, enthused by the excitement of Euro 96, got me to take them to Oakwell and the rest is a chequered history. Over the years we've seen promotions, relegations, cup runs, glorious wins and heavy defeats. The great thing about a sporting event, as I never tire of saying, is that you can often guess the end of a film or a play but you can rarely guess the end of a football match, and on the pitch you'll see courage, farce, comedy, tragedy and skill. And that's only in the warm up.

Barnsley F.C. have had, according to my reckoning, three finest hours. The first one was in 1912 when they beat West Bromwich Albion in a replay at Bramall Lane after a dour nil-nil draw was played at Crystal Palace. The replay was still nil-nil during extra time but Harry Tufnell's goal sealed a win and £49 1s 2d was collected for the Titanic Disaster Fund.

The second finest hour was in 1997 when a team managed by Danny Wilson passed and passed and passed and scored their way to the Premier League. On April 26th they beat Bradford City 2-0 with goals from Wilkinson and Marcelle to ascend to the Promised Land and 18,605 people were there, although if you talk to anybody who was alive in Barnsley at the time, and even a few who weren't, they'll say they were there so it becomes like the White Horse Final at Wembley or VE day in Leicester Square.

The third finest hour, or finest three hours, was in the Spring of 2016 when the team, managed by local lad ('He's one of our own' as we gleefully sing) Paul Heckingbottom visited Wembley twice to win the Johnstone's Paint Trophy and the League One Final. Tears of joy still prickle my eyes as I think about it.

I love to walk round Oakwell and, because I'm a fan of sports stadia, I like to marvel at the beauty of it. The East Stand rising and tubular like the Pompidou Centre in Paris, the North Stand like a huge monument to the money we got from selling Ashley Ward, the Ponty End that seems to channel the tiniest of chants into a mighty roar and the quaint old West Stand with its legendary facilities that give their name to the Barnsley Fanzine, *West Stand Bogs*.

LOCKE PARK

My Uncle Charlie, always one to coin a phrase or breathe life into a stale one, had a number of bons mots to hand if he found me staring out of the window. 'Tha stood theer like Souse!' he would say, or 'Tha stood theer like Clem!' or 'Tha stood theer like Joe Locke' pronounced Jooer Locke in the Barnsley way. Souse and Clem are lost in the mists of time but Jooer Locke refers not to, as Uncle Charlie thought, his favourite Irish tenor, but to the great nineteenth century railway engineer Joseph Locke.

Locke is the forgotten third of a triangle of men in tall hats who created the modern railway industry as we know it today, alongside Isambard Kingdom Brunel and George Stephenson. Locke's was a building-based and visionary imagination, seeing hills and valleys as possibilities for structural change and therefore cultural and social change. He designed much of what is now the West Coast mainline and one of his biggest triumphs, although at great human cost, was the Woodhead line between Sheffield and Manchester; indeed it was such a complex and difficult undertaking that Locke said that he'd eat the first locomotive that came out of the Woodhead Tunnel. It's not recorded if he did this or not. He was also the driver of Stephenson's Rocket on its maiden voyage in 1830 when it knocked down and killed the unfortunate Lord Huskisson.

Round here, though, Joe Locke is mainly remembered for none of these things; he is held in great affection in Barnsley because he gives his name to Locke Park on the northern edge of the town centre. His wife Phoebe gave the land to Barnsley in 1861 in memory of her husband; and it was opened in June 1862 and named 'The Peoples' Park' and these days functions as all town parks should, as a lung for the people of the tight streets. A vibrant Friends of Locke Park organises park runs and bonfires and galas, and opens the tower once a month (weather permitting, of course: you don't want to slip down the stairs like Lord Huskisson might have).

The tower is a fantastic folly which was commissioned by Phoebe's sister Sarah after Pheobe's death, and was opened in 1877. It was designed to combine a memorial and 'pleasure observatory' and it looks out over the bandstands and the fountain that make Locke Park such a joy to walk through and share. The tower was closed for a number of years from the 1990s due to safety concerns but the indefatigable Friends raised money to have it restored and it reopened in the autumn of 2013. The view from the tower on a clear day is spectacular and it makes you realise the full and resonant meaning of the words 'pleasure observatory' as you watch a park runner snatching a quick drag on a cig behind a bush where he thinks he can't be seen. You can talk about it in the café, which is also run by the friends, and you can raise a glass of pop to the memory of Joseph Locke and the park we wander round in his name.

MONK BRETTON

The constant surprise about Barnsley is that every now and then you come across something ancient, something that's just stood there for centuries letting the weather wash its face and dry its hands. These are buildings and places that couldn't care less that you're staring at them and making notes and taking photographs, and one of the greatest examples of these in the borough is Monk Bretton Priory, situated at Cundy Cross in Lundwood.

It's a twelfth century ecclesiastical building, originally set up by Cluniac monks as a sort of reserve bench for their main team near Pontefract Castle, although what English Heritage describe as 'gang wars' meant that it later set up on its own and became a Benedictine priory. I'm not a historian but I'm interested in the idea of orders of monks fighting gang wars, particularly if they were from a silent order. They had a market charter which was one of the reasons for Barnsley's rise as a market town and, if you believe in the 37 degrees of separation idea of history, it's thanks to these monks that you can buy black pudding on Barnsley Market.

The monks were amongst the first to mine coal in the area and according to local tales they would make their way in boats down the Dearne to Darfield to get their corn from the mill there. The Priory was trashed in 1538 after the dissolution of the monasteries and some of the stone was taken to be used for the new church in Wentworth, just a few miles away, and the bells were taken to London to be melted down. Nothing changes, I guess: things are nicked and the money trickles South. The Priory sits by the main road near houses and shops and takeaways but, and this is a cliché that just happens to be true, once you step into the area occupied by the Priory a kind of fragile peace descends. Even the visually and spatially illiterate like me (have you seen me trying to put up a tent? It's conceptual art) can get a sense of what the whole site would have been like in the sixteenth century. Places built around stone and light have almost been replaced by light but the stone still seems to stand there, invisible. There's hardly anything left of the church but luckily some of the other buildings are in a much better state of repair because people lived in them until the late 1800s and used the working toilets that were linked to the River Dearne.

I stand in the space of the ghost priory and imagine how it would have been as the Industrial Revolution grew up around it and the trains rattled by over the huge viaduct in Storrs Mill Wood and the road got busier and busier. I liken it to standing at Stonehenge and seeing the wagons rumble along to Salisbury.

The village of Monk Bretton got its name from the Priory, being referred to as Munkebretton in 1225; the medieval butter cross is one of the oldest parts of the village and it's well worth a look but care must be taken (to use a guidebook phrase) because it stands on the junction of two busy roads. Even though Monk Bretton is an ancient settlement, there aren't that many preserved older buildings, and as a fan of follies I have to say that one particular loss I feel keenly is Monk Bretton Castle, a remarkable tower structure that was built by a local clergyman, Mr Wordsworth, and was used as a lookout tower and beacons were lit there to mark special occasions. I never saw it but the one photograph I've seen gives it a dark grandeur.

St Paul's Church is where I often rang the bells as a teenager with the help of the nominatively-determined Ted Bell. Given the extreme age of the settlement, it's unusual that the church is a relatively recent one being built in 1838. Inside, you can see a carving of the amazing-looking 'Madonna of the Working Classes'.

The pit at Monk Bretton opened in 1870 and closed in 1968, before the huge wave of pit closures after the 1984-85 strike; there's nothing left of it now but a stroll along the scrubland where it used to be.

I'm always looking for metaphor in landscape and place, and I found one round here once when my grandson's cricket club played Monk Bretton one still June evening. One of the great advantages of watching him play football and cricket is that it takes me to parts of Barnsley I've never visited before. The recreation ground at the back of the houses in Worsbrough. The high fields at the back of the old Boys Grammar School where the wind attacks you with bread knives. The field at Hoyland Common where the Zumba music is a constant soundtrack. The field at Darton that you find down a track by the sound of people shouting 'That wor nivver a penalty, ref!' The Cricket Club at Monk Bretton is at the back of a pub called the Pheasant and you get a fantastic view over Barnsley's lines of streets and the Oakwell's stands and floodlights.

My wife and I arrived to find the team standing outside the locked gate of the cricket club, looking like chesspieces with boxes on. We hung around like monks waiting for the sound of the Dissolution to come cantering over the hill. The phone rang and the trainer told us the Monk Bretton team had gone to Darfield and were standing around the edge of the field like resting morris dancers with shin pads on. It was agreed that we should go back to Darfield to play the match but still, according to a Heath Robinson version of the rules, treat it as an away fixture. We piled into our cars like cops in a HBO show and were about to set off, indeed the lead cars had already left, when the trainer waved us back because Monk Bretton were on their way. That's like me, looking for psychogeographical truth in one site and then learning that it might be located on another field but then being sent back to the first field again.

I could walk to or from a lot of the places round here and I'd end up at Stairfoot Roundabout, a place notorious in Barnsley folklore since it was built in the 1980s. An easy way to start a conversation in Barnsley is just to say, in the pub or on the bus, 'Eee, it was busy at Stairfoot Roundabout this morning' and then sit back and let the stories flood in. Have a notebook or recording device handy. The 'Eee' is optional, by the way, but the natives like it and it will establish you as a friendly person. It's the oral equivalent of sparkly trinkets.

Stairfoot Roundabout has been immortalised in song by local artist and musician Dave Cherry and in some ways the roundabout stands as a symbol for any disliked modernisation in any town anywhere. Taxi drivers will always tell you that the roundabout works better when the lights aren't working, because after all that's the function of roundabouts.

Near the roundabout towards Hunningley School there's an area that used to be called Sodom, presumably because it was, to use travel agents' language, 'lively', and older people still refer to the area as 'Sodom' or sometimes as 'Sodom and Gomorrah.' I'm fascinated by these folk names to places that persist like ghosts hanging around behind the official maps. An area near John Street was known as New Guinea and there's a part of town called, evocatively 'Bare Bones', or 'Bare Booans', near the town centre where the weavers' cottages were in the eighteenth and nineteenth centuries. Some people believe that Bare Bones refers to the extreme poverty suffered by people in the area but Dave Cherry and others believe that it's an almost poetic allusion to the fact that the public gibbet was in the area and that swinging bodies would stay there until they were picked clean to the bare booans. I like that interpretation.

NEW LODGE AND ATHERSLEY

I like functional place names or names that appear on the surface to be functional; there's Nome in Alaska which was supposedly called that because a dozing cartographer, presumably thinking about his tea, was meant to write down the word Name because they didn't know the name of the settlement, but instead wrote Nome, which is what it became. That's an accidental functionality, I guess, but there's a real functionality to all those places called Intake, and the town of Stockport.

Well, in Barnsley, I've always thought New Lodge was one heck of a functional name. It's a new estate full of lodgings so let's call it New Lodge. Well, that's a little of the story. The area of New Lodge was originally farmland but a huge number of council houses were built there in the 1940s and 1950s to house the families who supplied the workforce for the local mines and factories. A number of the houses were of the distinctive post-war type known as Tarran Houses which were an American design and because they were made of metal, they would rattle like a can of marbles and possibly blow away in a gale, like Dorothy's house in *The Wizard of Oz*. In fact they were often sturdy and warm and the people who lived in them often swore they'd never live anywhere else.

The pre-New Lodge area has a fascinating history; in the mid-nineteenth century maps show a scattering of farmhouses in the area, a manor house which is now a private care home, and the Roundhouse Lodge which was a very unusual eight-sided building that was (and isn't this often the story of this book and of the other books in this series?) demolished in the mid-1960s. The Roundhouse lives on in local folklore and long memory and in the name of the local medical centre. Photographs of the Roundhouse show an imposing structure that would have dominated the main road to Wakefield, as a gatehouse to the Manor Farm.

Coterminous with New Lodge is Athersley, divided into two areas, North and South; like New Lodge it was once All Fields Round Here but in the 1940s it was developed to house Barnsley's growing population; all that separates Athersley North and Athersley South is Laithes Lane, but don't tell the people of Athersley North or Athersley South that. The local pit was the enormous Wharncliffe Woodmoor Colliery which was initially sunk in 1871 and closed in 1966 during yet another government scheme of accelerated pit closures.

Although I know that there is nothing remotely poetic about the sheer hard back-breaking graft of being a miner, there is something resonant about the names of the seams that were worked from Wharncliffe Woodmoor: Haigh Moor, Barnsley, Kent's Thick, Winter, Lidgett and Beamshaw. In August 1936 an explosion in the Lidgett seam killed 58 miners, ripping the local community to pieces, and was the worst mining disaster in South Yorkshire in modern times. There's a moving memorial to the people who lost their lives at the entrance to Wharncliffe Business Park. Business parks aren't really the territory of books like this, but places like this one and the factories and warehouses alongside the main road between Darfield and Grimethorpe are the future of towns like Barnsley, and I think we should celebrate them by remembering the past but facing towards the future. I sing the body pre-fabricated, as Walt Whitman might have sung if he'd lived round here.

Carlton is the third of a triumvirate with New Lodge and Athersley, and is always associated in the lives of my children when they were small with the idea of ten pin bowling at Barnsley Bowl. The first time we took them, on a rainy Sunday afternoon that happened to be somebody's birthday, I thought I'd stumbled into the first five minutes of an American independent film fresh from Sundance. There was the echoing noise of the skittles (is that the right word? Probably not) and the squeak of the shoes that you hired and the laughter of the families and I expected the Fonz to appear at any moment from his New Lodge pied-à-terre. Barnsley Bowl is still there, still going strong, and well worth a visit for a strike or a spare.

In this part of Barnsley I always get a real sense of the borough as a number of different villages, often built around a pit or near to a pit, often self-contained, often with their own separate councils until a generation ago, each with a sense of fierce local pride and often, unless you have a delivery business or relatives in the area or a local football match to go to, not visited by people from any of the villages at the other end of the borough. Why go to Jump from Shafton? Why go to Oxspring from Thurnscoe? You tell me, my friend. But I think you should.

Another attraction in Carlton is Carlton Marsh (not Carlton Marshes, that's in Suffolk) a beautiful nature reserve, declared as such in the early 1980s when the rest of Barnsley's infrastructure was about to experience severe strain and perhaps start to fall to pieces, placed damply between Carlton, Shafton, Royston and Cudworth and serving as a green lung for all those settlements. On a clear evening or a spring morning, you can spot bird-spotters spotting birds and people walking and children running and laughing almost as though they're taking part in a promotional film. In a recent Yorkshire in Bloom competition Carlton Marsh won gold, deservedly. I always think a dragonfly on the wing is a good sign of nature being in rude health, and last time I was there one zoomed by, as big as a World War One fighter plane. I ducked, but I ducked with a sense of satisfaction.

MAPPLEWELL AND STAINCROSS

There are so many places in Barnsley (and beyond, I realise) that I could say this about, but don't ever say that a Mapplewell person is from Staincross and vice versa. As far as the citizens of these two places are concerned, well, you may as well call them the village of

Chalk and the village of Cheese. Indeed, in 2003, the inhabitants of Staincross, led by local man and universally-known cricket umpire Harold 'Dickie' Bird, held a Swiss-style local ballot to determine whether their address should be Staincross or Mapplewell or, heaven forbid, Darton. The Staincrossites voted overwhelmingly by 966 to 199 to keep their envelope-based independence and the Royal Mail bowed to their wishes. Owzat!

It's true that they have certain similarities in that they were both central to the growth of nailmaking in and around Barnsley in the eighteenth and nineteenth centuries; it began as most of these industries did with people working from home making their own implements for repair work. Making nails was a secondary activity to farm work, when there was little to do in the winter months when there was less farm work to be completed. By 1841 there were 244 nailmakers in Staincross and Mapplewell and 45 miners, but by 1861 there were 280 nailmakers and 314 miners. Early smaller pits were replaced by the huge North Gawber Pit in Mapplewell which was sunk in 1850 and eventually closed in 1987.

JUNCTION 37

Junction 37 is the main junction off the M1 into Barnsley, although with my Darfield bias I wonder they don't call it Barnsley North in the same way that they call Junction 36 Barnsley South. Don't get me started.

Junction 37 is a roundabout with a commanding view of the motorway and the surrounding countryside; coming north you turn right into Barnsley and left to get to the A628 and eventually over the borough's empty moorland and on to Manchester. At first sight there seems to be less hinterland to Junction 37 although there's at least one magnificent feral apple tree on the grassland to the left of the roundabout and this one is surviving and thriving, unlike the one at Junction 36.

Just off the roundabout on the Dodworth side there's a pub, the Dodworth Valley, and a hotel. The Dodworth Valley is a Toby Carvery and its strapline is 'the home of the roast', which suits Barnsley people very well because it's always busy. The hotel behind it, which at the moment is an Ibis, but has been other things in its time, is one of a number of hotels clustered around the junction, with the Bluebell a bit down the road and the Holiday Inn just a little further away in Dodworth. I'm not sure that there's a valley nearby, in the same way that there isn't a farm near the Dearne Valley Farm

If I'm ever, as I often am, in a chain hotel I always take a stroll around the area just to try and work out what the hotel has been placed on top of. At the Ibis at Junction 37 you wouldn't have to walk too far to get the full majesty of the M1, a 24-hour soundtrack that ebbs and flows but never completely fades away. You could carefully cross the roads and wander a little way down Dodworth Road towards town; there are houses on the right with long gardens that face idyllic fields, and on the left there's a very unusual modernist cubic, flat-roofed house called Four Corners which is well worth glancing at as you wander by. Dodworth Road is one of the main arteries into and out of Barnsley, and gets very busy as fortunate people try to rush into town and less fortunate people try to rush out.

Back from the hotel is Capitol Park, a new business park on the edge of Dodworth. It was built in 2007, just after the time when it seemed that the money would go on forever and the day of reckoning would never arrive. It's built in a confident style, seemingly constructed from the sounds of fast cars on motorways and the rustle of business deals being concluded on a handshake. Places like this are as much a part of Barnsley as the Italianate church at Goldthorpe and so they must be gazed at and taken in, even though many of them look the same.

For a while there was a rumour that a huge statue of a miner, in the style of The Angel of the North, was to be put up on the roundabout, but that came to nothing. In the end that's probably not a bad thing because we should look forward more than we look back or maybe we should, as I've suggested more than once in this book, look both ways at once.

THE MINERS' STRIKE

If I walk up past the Cooper Gallery and the statue of Dickie Bird, cross the road and stroll to the bottom of Huddersfield Road, I come to the NUM Building with its poignant and moving Graham Ibbeson statue of a grieving mining family outside, with the inscription 'In memory of those who have lost their lives in supporting their union in times of struggle'. In the heyday of the

NUM this magnificent building was known as King Arthur's Castle after the miners' leader Arthur Scargill. The building itself is sometimes open on heritage open days and is well worth a look round. The miners' strike is Barnsley's recent defining moment; it was the event that changed the town forever, and forced it to rethink its role and try to work out how it might go forward. As an old councillor said to me once 'Tha can't just lay down and dee.' Which is true.

Let's just consider for a moment how many coal mines there were in the Barnsley Borough as the strike began: Barnsley Main, Darfield, Cortonwood, Dearne Valley, Dodworth, Goldthorpe, Grimethorpe, Hickleton, Houghton Main, North Gawber and Royston. All these pits have now gone, together with the infrastructure and the collectivism and the solidarity that went with them. Thousands of people employed directly and indirectly; families working down the pit but always saying that their lads would never work down the pit, that they'd go on to something else, something better, and now they never can.

As I write this, in the spring of 2017, there are hardly any visual reminders of the huge structures that made this place tick. Muckstacks are grassed over and pithead gear has gone. Pit wheels or representations of pit wheels dot roundabouts and at places like Skiers Springs near Hoyland, old mining sheds have been put to other use, in this case as a garage. The most visual memory is the Barnsley Main winding gear, suddenly appearing as you drive away from Oakwell, a site for fly-tipping but lovingly cleaned every now and then by volunteers who understand the significance of glancing back while staring resolutely straight ahead.

In a parallel world where the strike was won by the union somebody called Ian McMillan is writing a book called *Real Barnsley* and things are very different. Several pits are still open; there's an air of quiet prosperity. There are shops and they are full. There are parks and they are loved. There is a sense of purpose, a sense that the place is a kind of engine room, an R&D lab, a workshop for the world. That's the parallel world, of course. Not this one. When you visit us here as a result of reading this book, try and imagine the place as it was before all the pits went, before the deliberate destruction of the mining industry. Try and imagine it before the pits came, too. Imagine those pasts and then visit the present.

A Deep Tarn Calendar – April

Sumbdy at dooor. Knock knockin
Like a crap joooak. April fooil.
Am not guin. It'll be kidz
Knock knockin. Like a crap jooak.
Phooan ringin. Phooan ringin
Like start on a telly detective.
Am norranswerin. It'll bi sumbdy
Tranner sell mi summat.
April fooil. Not me. Not me pal.
Keep knockin. Keep ringin.

A Deep Tarn Calendar – May

Might not need a vesser.
Today I might be a feller
Ooo dunt need a vesser.
Bit warmer missis.
Tha waint need a cardi
Well tha might need a cardi
An I might beed a vesser
Cos tha can nivver tell
At this time of year
Pass that vesser ovver here
An I'll gi thi thi cardi.

A Deep Tarn Calendar – June

Leet all neet
Dunt need a neet leet
Cos its leet all neet
Completely leet
Tha can sit on thi seat
And read bi't leet
From't sky all neet.
After midneet
That might gerra semmas
What tha might call
A soorta
Diminution
A tha noz
Dilution
On leet
But then it gets leet
Completely leet.

WEST

CAWTHORNE AND SILKSTONE

Whenever Barnsley F.C. get further than expected in the FA Cup, or are about to get promoted or relegated, film crews will always be despatched to film the (ahem) real Barnsley, and the shot they'll almost always use is one of the pithead gear at Barnsley Main. If an old bloke in a flat cap is walking by then that's a bonus. Get some library brass band music to underlay it and Bob's your Barnsley uncle.

What these TV types never do is go to Cawthorne because in their eyes Cawthorne, or Silkstone or Hoylandswaine or High Hoyland are not ur-Barnsley. Well, I'm here to tell you that they are.

The jewel in the crown of this end of Barnsley is the amazing Cannon Hall, one of our many big houses (see almost any other page of this book), but one that has survived and thrived as a national tourist attraction with, as a bonus, one of the best collections of pear trees you'll ever see[1], a farm shop with lustrous pies and a café that does afternoon teas that include little Yorkshire puddings, which is my kind of afternoon tea.

It's a huge house owned and extended by the Spencer, later the Spencer-Stanhope, family, from an earlier thirteenth-century house built by one Gilbert Canun, who gave the house its name. The Spencer-Stanhopes created the essence of the place we now know in the eighteenth century which is beautiful and yet not remote; perhaps because it's in Barnsley it seems to feel like it belongs to the crowds who throng around it all the time. The last member of the family, Elizabeth, sold the house to Barnsley Council in 1951 and it opened to the public in 1957.

When I was younger it certainly felt that Cannon Hall was a bit dusty and a little remote but these days, thanks to the efforts of the indefatigable Friends of Cannon Hall and the council, it really is open to all in a way that might have made a member of the Spencer-Stanhope family twitch a little and arrange his face slowly into a rictus grin. As I write this Cannon Hall has just been awarded nearly three million pounds by the National Lottery to restore the gardens to their natural glory and I for one can't wait to see people pouring off trains and getting out of buses to marvel at them and to spend their quids in the farm shop. Mind you, I read in the *Barnsley Chronicle* the other day that the Chipping Sodbury Branch of the Retired Tesco Workers Association had visited Barnsley. They're coming!

When I've marvelled at Cannon Hall, I have a look around the farm and the farm shop; then I watch a bit of ferret racing and goat milking and settle down and get to know a pie from the outside in. As a child, I never thought about anybody actually coming to Barnsley as tourists or visitors, whether the town centre or places like Cannon Hall. As a young man I witnessed the first flowering of the post-industrial tourist economy and, even though I'd been to places like Coalbrookdale and Telford and seen the posters for 'Bradford: A Surprising Place' I still felt a little uneasy about the concept of people coming to my town, my village, as tourists, even though I was part of that economy by making a cassette (yes, a cassette) tour of Barnsley and Wakefield industrial heritage[2]. Now that I'm a man in late middle-age I get the idea and I'm getting more excited about the possibilities. Maybe it takes that long for the shockwaves of the stripping out of the industrial base to subside and for the dust to clear before you can really see where you are and where you're going. Cannon Hall will do for a start, on a Spring Sunday. Don't forget the pies.

As a village, Cawthorne is a kind of adjunct to Cannon Hall; as the village website says, it's the kind of place that estate agents talk of as 'much sought after' but if you dig a little deeper you can trip over history and try it on for size. Cawthorne wears the architectural and topographical tattoos of two important families, the Barnbys and the aforementioned Spencer-Stanhopes in buildings like the Barnby Hall and the Spencer Arms. There are the

remains of a canal basin at Cawthorne, which was the end of the
Barnsley Canal, and where coal was brought by horse-drawn trams
along the Waggon Road from Silkstone and lime was burned in
kilns.

All Saints' Church dates in part from the early thirteenth century
and is the kind of place you can lose yourself in, feeling the
influence of the moneyed families of the village in the tombs and
inscriptions and stained glass windows and in the changing and
unchanging seasons of the community. There are six bells in the
tower and I have a vague memory of ringing them one weekend in
the 1970s and being caught up in a rope and briefly flung around
the ringing chamber as though weightless. It may have been
another tower in the area, though: I was weightless in many of
them, briefly.

One of the jewels in Cawthorne's considerable crown is the
Jubilee Museum[3]. The Cawthorne Museum Society was formed in
1884 by the first-line-of-a-limerick-waiting-to-happen Reverend
Charles Tiplady Pratt who was one of those Victorian vicars who
hoped to catch the Lord in his net but ending up snaring butterflies
and eggs and fossils. He encouraged the formation of groups to
study natural history, astronomy and the weather and eventually his
collections outgrew the old cottage they were housed in and he
convinced Walter Spencer-Stanhope and his artist brother Roddam
to demolish the cottage and the one next door an create a
purpose-built museum which was officially opened in 1889 with,
'scenes of great rejoicing, plus a public tea – White Tickets at 5pm

and Red Tickets at 5.45pm. It is requested that persons with Red Tickets do not try to take tea at 5pm. Rev C.T. Pratt.'

When Cannon Hall was sold to Barnsley Council for use as a museum, the Cannon Hall Estate sold the Victoria Jubilee Museum to the village for £100, in a kind of pre-echo of the way Maurice Dobson's house was acquired by the Darfield Amenities Society to create a museum. The Cawthorne Museum continued to grow and a new extension was opened in April 1983 by the Lord Bishop of Wakefield and, in a marvellous example of symmetry tea was held in the village hall just as it had been a hundred years before but this time tickets were the same colour and everyone had tea at the same time which for me is a little disappointing; I'd have liked to see the Red Ticket/White Ticket rule still in force.

The Jubilee Museum itself is a proper Victorian museum with an avalanche of exhibits, each of which could detain you for ages and make you miss your red-ticket tea. There's a huge gallstone from a horse as well as a sculpture of John Wesley made from a whale's vertebra as well as coins, medals and a mantrap. The Trustees who run the museum say, and I agree with them, that it's the only survivor of John Ruskin's dream of a network of village museums set up and thriving all over the country.

A big change occurred in the village during World War Two when an army camp took over part of Cannon Hall and opencast mining crept across much of Cawthorne removing a nine-hole golf course, an open air swimming pool and an old cricket field. After the war the Cannon Hall Camp became a centre for Polish soldiers and their families as a resettlement camp until 1952. There's a plaque in the village to mark the camp and its important role on the history of Cawthorne, something that perhaps the casual visitor to Cannon Hall and the farm shop wouldn't normally think about. Those who think of Cawthorne simply as an old estate village untouched by the Industrial Revolution and the turbulence of the twentieth century should take their time and look around. And visit the Jubilee Museum. And then go and have something to eat in the Spencer Arms.[4]

As a young sensitive poetic type I remember writing the name Silkstone over and over again in a notebook, sometimes splitting it into its two component parts Silk and Stone. I showed the minimalist list to my English teacher Mr Brown and said 'What do you think of my concrete poem?'. He smiled indulgently and put it in his briefcase. I'm not sure where it ended up after that.

There's something about the Silk and the Stone about Silkstone and Silkstone Common. Silkstone is an old farming village mentioned in the Domesday Book and was also a centre of coalmining, with a number of pits in the Silkstone Valley which transported their coal to the canal at Cawthorne via the Silkstone Waggonway[5].

There had been coal mined in the area for centuries but the coalfield really expanded, as most of them did, with the coming of the railways and canals. A good way to explore the area is to take the Waggonway Trail; in the way that old names hang on, the bridleway through Silkstone is locally known as The Waggonway for ways perhaps not always understood, like Cat Hill in Darfield.

The Penistone website recommends that you start your trail at Silkstone Common railway station; the present station was opened in 1983 along with Dodworth Station when the Huddersfield to Sheffield line was restored and upgraded. The new station is on the site of the old station which closed in 1959. The station is built over the tunnel that the Waggonway came along; the untrained eye can't spot much evidence of the Waggonway, although I've tried many times as the train chugged in wait for signals to change.

The Waggonway and the inclined plane from Moorend at the top of the Dove Valley and the self-acting Inclined Plane near the site of the 1930 Black Horse Tunnel are remarkable feats of engineering. When wagons had been brought through the tunnel by horses they were connected to a brake-checking drum to control their descent; to make sure they didn't roll away down the hill causing injury and losing money they were counterbalanced by eight empty wagons were pulled up at the same time the full ones descended. I've just written it down and I can't quite understand it either but if you stand there looking, you can just about work it out.

In Nabs Wood nearby I stand and gaze at the very moving memorial to the Huskar Pit disaster of 1838 in which 26 children aged from seven to seventeen drowned after heavy rainfall disabled the winding engine and the miners were told to wait at the pit bottom to be rescued. The children, bravely and foolishly, decided to try to escape via a nearby day-pit in the wood; most of them never saw the daylight again. The memorial, which was built in 1988 to mark the 150th anniversary of the disaster, shows two children trying to escape, or perhaps simply working, on their hands and knees in a mine's cramped tunnel. I first came across the memorial by accident, and perhaps that's the best way to find it, on a misty morning when the past and the present seem to be wearing the same shirt; one that doesn't quite fit. The children were buried in the churchyard at All Saints in Silkstone, and an almost unbearably moving stone lists their names and ages.

PENISTONE

The first thing that people from Penistone will tell you is that it's not in Barnsley, definitely not. The second thing that people from Penistone will tell you is that it's most certainly not part of Sheffield. The third thing people from Penistone will tell you is that the best way to approach it is over the viaduct on the train from Denby Dale when, on a sunny day, it really does seem like you're flying across the fields as the shadow of your carriage floats over the grass and the sheep[6]. And you're nowhere near Sheffield, nowhere near Barnsley.

It's true that Penistone is a place on its own, a proper separate town reputed to be the highest market town in England. It really does feel like a little independent city-state within the Borough of Barnsley. The town bills itself as 'The Pennine Heart of South Yorkshire' a clever slice of marketing that avoids the use of the B-word or the S-word but emphasises the Y-word.

It would be good if the train I visited Penistone on was a music train; there aren't as many music trains as there used to be, but in the past there have been folk trains, bluegrass trains, jazz trains and opera trains. People board the train at Sheffield and listen and sing and glug real ale and sometimes forget to get off and sometimes get off at the wrong stop singing coal-mining ballads or arias from *Turandot*. My favourite part of any music train is the reactions of baffled commuters who first think they've stumbled on a carriage full of football drunks until they see their first banjo. Later in the journey you see them, ties tied round their head like Willie Nelson's bandana, joining in the songs even though they don't know the words or the tune or eventually their own name and address.

A number of years ago I led a poetry train on the line as part of the Huddersfield Literature Festival which was a mixed success, I have to say[7]. The idea was that there would be readings and workshops and perhaps a rendition of W.H. Auden's 'Night Mail'. We boarded (or barded) at Huddersfield and the first thing I noticed was that there was no microphone. The ancient pacer trains used on the line rattle so much that even on a fairly smooth section of track they sound like a man in armour falling down several flights of stairs so the chances of reciting deathless verse were limited unless your voice was even louder than mine. I asked about the microphone and was told it would be boarding at Penistone, presumably not on its own with a special Microphone Day Rover. I guess that these days we could have used some kind of wireless technology but, as I remember (it was a very long time ago and I didn't keep detailed notes or any notes because the train was shaking too much) the ancient sound equipment was accompanied by a man who had, to employ a euphemism, sucked too hard at the Ambrosia Nipples of the Gods. He had to be helped into the carriage and left the wire for the microphone to wait for the next train.

I often say to TV producers when I meet them on my dizzying media whirl that if I'm ever asked to make a programme about Great Railway Journeys of the World, I will choose this line. It's a survivor, having almost been closed in the early 1980s, and now it's a busy artery between villages, towns and cities, used by shoppers and commuters, and a number of new stations have been opened, including Dodworth and Silkstone Common within the geographical boundaries that this book covers.

If I get off the train at Penistone I always stroll to the Paramount Cinema, another great survivor[8]. It was built as a public hall in 1914 (or as a library in 1913, according to some sources), showed its first films in 1915, and it's been showing them ever since. There aren't many single-space picture palaces left but the Paramount is a fantastic example of a community cinema that really works. The

USP of the Paramount Cinema, it seems to me (and the clue is in the name) is the mighty Compton organ that was built in 1937 for the Paramount Theatre in Birmingham. When that Paramount closed the organ was moved to a cinema in Oswestry, and when that closed its doors for the last time, the organ was brought by Kevin Grunhill[9], the enthusiastic Penistone keyboard-wizard. It was kept in storage for a number of years and eventually restored and given pride of place in what was then called the Metro Cinema but which was renamed the Paramount Cinema in honour of the organ. Which is a nice touch, and a bit like calling a guitar venue the Fender.

There are monthly organ concerts (don't call them recitals, whatever you do) at the Paramount, which are joyous communions of people who often get bracketed with trainspotters or bellringers as Great British Eccentrics but who are simply people who love skill and musicianship and a good tune played very very loudly. I once did a gig at the Paramount with my band, the modestly-named Ian McMillan Orchestra, and I can testify to the majesty and power of the huge space. My grandson, then a small child, came and sat on the front row and said afterwards that his favourite bit was that he could see me in the bit off the stage waiting to come on. I think I'll introduce him to *Waiting for Godot* when he's a bit older. It'll be his empty cup of tea with no saucer.

My son-in-law talked about visiting Penistone for a beer-swilling session with his mates and they wanted to go on the train and get dressed up as, as they put it, 'People from Penistone'. They decided they would wear tweed jackets and flat caps and cravats. I don't agree with this stereotype, of course, but that's an indication of how different and unique Penistone is within the urban/suburban/rural ecology of the Barnsley Borough. As far as many people are concerned, it wears a cravat, even to an organ concert. Of course we know that's not true. It's a bow tie.

The first time I visited Penistone was to ring bells. As a bearded teenager I was a bellringer; never a campanologist, always a bellringer. For many years my geography of Barnsley and the surrounding area was defined by bell-towers in a way that would have made Walter Benjamin or Georges Perec proud. My home village of Darfield was a ring of six bells, lovingly restored eventually to eight after the NCB (the other agency that defines this town alongside Earl Fitzwilliam from Wentworth) agreed to pay for the damage caused by the shafts that snaked under the church, rendering it unstable. Monk Bretton had six bells and there was a link between Monk Bretton and Penistone that could stump many a team at a local history pub quiz, even the ones who knew the name of the goal-scorer in Barnsley's famous FA Cup win. Harry Tufnell[10].

The link, of course, is Yorkshire Tail Ends. Yorkshire Tail Ends on your sally. St John's Church at Penistone, when I rang the bells there in the late 1970s, had Yorkshire Tail Ends. A sally is the coloured bit on a bellrope that looks a bit like the pole outside a retro barber's. Normally the sally is halfway up the rope and it helps you grip, but in a few churches the end of the rope is also made from the coloured rope and this is called a Yorkshire Tail End. My tiny, soft poet's hands didn't like the Yorkshire Tail Ends; you needed hands like coal scuttles to be able to grip them properly. It would be good for cinema organ players, I guess; you could stretch your fingers over a number of octaves.

St John's Church is just up the hill from the Paramount Cinema and the tower has been there since the sixteenth century. It's an imposing building, showing the historic and contemporary importance of Penistone as a farming centre, although the Domesday Book describes it as 'waste'. Livestock has been sold in the market for hundreds of years and a market charter was awarded in 1699. As with many towns of this size and vintage, it was the coming of the railway that led to a sudden increase in the population and the building of the aforementioned 29-arch viaduct (built with local stone brought along a tramway) that brings you into the town. Penistone was a busy junction with trains to Sheffield, Manchester and Huddersfield, until Dr Beeching tolled his bell (without a Yorkshire Tail End) and the Woodhead line shut and the station is now a once-an-hour each way brace of platforms to Huddersfield or Sheffield.

I was once on the last train from Huddersfield to Barnsley; it wasn't officially a music train although nobody told the man in front of me because he was busy making his way through the Greatest Hits of Elvis Presley. At Penistone a man got on and looked at the singing bloke. 'Now or nivver is it?' The new arrival looked at me: 'Buffet car, kid?' he asked, as though I was an employee of Northern Rail. The Elvis Man launched into

'Suspicious Minds'. I shook my head. 'No buffet car?' the man said. He pointed at the singer. 'Ah well, at least we've got cabaret.'

THURLSTONE AND THURGOLAND

When I was a child I loved the names of the villages of Thurlstone and Thurgoland. They felt like twin Viking brothers, one wild and ready to fight you at the drop of a horned hat, one gentle and full of poems and sagas. Thurlstone was the gentle one. His lyre (or whatever the Viking equivalent was) was tuned and ready to play, and the wine in his cup was more like fizzy pop. Thurgoland was a warrior from the Land of the Thurgos who would be no good at all on the top deck of the bus from Barnsley because he'd be swinging his sword around his head as though he was pretending to be a helicopter. I realise that none of this is historically or culturally accurate but I was, as I said, a child at the time.

The reality is that neither of these villages are like a mighty warrior, and both of them are more likely to carry a lyre than a flaming torch. Mind you, I could have been fairly close to the truth with the origin of Thurgoland because the name is an Old Norse one and may mean 'cultivated land of a man called Thorgeirr' and a man with Geirr in his name could be fierce, or he could be saying the Old Yorkshire word 'Geeor' which means 'Please stop'. Thurgoland has a number of historical claims to fame, the oddest of which is that a railway station opened there in 1845 but closed less than a year later, although there was a mineral line serving the nearby Stanhope Silkstone Main Colliery. I'm disturbed and unsettled by any station closure but closing one after two months seems particularly quixotic, just as people are building it into their daily routines. It's like cutting down a washing line just when you've got used to hanging your pants on it.

Thurgoland's main industry was wire drawing[11], the process of shrinking the beginning of a length of wire so that the rest of the wire could be pulled through a die. A modern example of something created by wire drawing is telephone wire which is drawn from hot rolled stock. There were three wire mills in Thurgoland, the oldest dating from the seventeenth century. If you're looking for an example of those big houses that dominate and define the Barnsley landscape[12], then you don't need to look any further than Huthwaite Hall, which was built for the owner of the Wortley Ironworks, John Cockshutt (stop giggling at the back).

Wire drawers would have been thirsty people because there have in recent times been four pubs in Thurlstone, which is a lot per head in a small village. The Monkey, which was the equivalent of a Restoration Coffee Shop with beer, was a hotbed of poetry and art, with sculptures in the car park, but closed a few years ago. Crane Moor, which melts into Thurgoland, used to be a mining village with, according to the parish website, five pubs, a street of shops and a brace of Methodist chapels.

Thurlstone is a small village on the edge of Penistone that was famous when I was younger for its handbells. As a ringer of church bells you often had to be versatile enough to turn your hand (!) to handbells although it was a very different skill, like being expected to be able to knit a jumper just because you were good at playing the trombone. The Darfield Handbell Ringers would clank out a few carols at Christmas that, because of my lack of hand-eye co-ordination, sounded like a drunk ringing a broken doorbell, and out leader Mike King would always tell us that one day we might be as good as the Thurlstone Bell Orchestra who could not only hold a tune but could hold two bells in each hand, making a note as the hand moved up and a different note as the hand moved down.

The Thurlstone Handbell Ringers were formed in 1855 at the Sunday School, and a contemporary photograph shows a row of men sitting round a table on which the handbells are displayed like trophies. They look less like handbell ringers than rugby union players, although everybody looked older and tougher then, because it was The Past. I remember doing a joint concert with Thurlstone once and it felt like we were a tribute band in the presence of the real thing, Noasis on the same stage as Oasis. Rumour has it that although the Thurlstone Handbells still exist, they are no longer being rung which is a terrible shame because if a bell is not rung it's simply a metal daffodil, as the old Thurlstone saying goes.

The small but beatifically formed St Saviour's Church[13], on the main Manchester road between Thurlstone and Millhouse Green, is a splendid example of local philanthropy, and of the fingers of the local gentry finding their way into many pies. The church was built at the beginning of the twentieth century with a legacy given by the sisters Mary and Hannah Bray on land given by Mr Thomasson of Plumpton House, and the foundation stone was laid by Sir Walter Spencer-Stanhope from Cannon Hall. The church cost £7500 and I've always found it odd and poignant that although a tower was going to be built, they ran out of money before it could be started. A local man gave a single bell which, in a village famous for its handbells, seems a little sad, a touch ironic. The beautiful carved wooden screen behind the altar is notable because it's one of the few that I've come across that's been carved by a woman; in this case Clara Nokes, the sister-in-law to the first vicar.

I realise, as I write this book, that churches feature a lot; I'm not a religious man, although as I said in the Darfield chapter, I did go to church twice every Sunday when I was a boy. The more I travel around Barnsley borough, in widening circles away from Darfield, the more I realise that, alongside the big house and the pit, the church building is one more important layer of history, the third side of the triangle, the third point on the compass.

I could plot a trip round Barnsley via its churches, starting on the edge of town with the Reverend Tiverton Preedy's St Paul's and ending up here in Thurlstone. On the way you'd encounter piety and vanity and a range of architecture and craftsmen and women that would give you a view of the borough as a cultural and artistic centre.

One of Thurlstone's almost forgotten sons is Nicholas Saunderson, who was blinded by smallpox as a boy but went on to become a professor of mathematics at Cambridge[14]. He's almost forgotten but not quite: musician and head teacher Andy Platt who is from Thurlstone and is passionate about bringing Saunderson's story to a wider audience, wrote a musical about him called *No Horizon*, which was performed locally and enjoyed a successful run at the 2016 Edinburgh Fringe. The story is a remarkable rags-to-maths story, made all the more incredible by Saunderson's blindness.

STAINBOROUGH

There are parts of the borough that feel special in a personal way and which feel different and exciting in a political and topographical way. As a young man, freshly dropped into the world of the freelance writer and performer in the early 1980s, I spent many hours running writing workshops at Northern College in Stainborough, a village just to the north of Barnsley.

In the past Northern College had been Wentworth Castle College, a teacher training college for women which specialised, so the rumour went, in Domestic Science, and that each girl was presented with an apron on their first day. Ah, so very long ago and so very far away!

Wentworth Castle College closed in 1978 and eventually became Northern College[15], an adult education residential college for people who had missed out at school and who wanted to get qualifications to gain entry to universities and what we used to call polytechnics. I took informal poetry classes in the bar with a mixed bag of students including a bloke who always insisted on performing 'Dangerous Dan McGrew', a person known affectionately as the Accrington Rat, a learned lecturer called Bob who translated poems from the Spanish and Brian Sefton[16], one of the leading lights of Barnsley's literary scene for many years. Somehow, in that radical room, it felt like we were taking back something that belonged to us, writing our poems in the bowels of the gentry's domain.

Wentworth Castle was yet another of the huge houses that dominate this part of Yorkshire, but the story of this one is intriguing and addictive. In the late seventeenth century Thomas Wentworth fully expected to inherit the breathtaking estate at Wentworth Woodhouse, the longest single-fronted house in Europe, which frankly makes Wentworth Castle, amazing as it is, look like a doll's house, on the death of the second Earl of Strafford. Thomas didn't get his hands on the estate or the house because they went to the Earl's cousin, another Thomas, so he decided to create his own.

In 1708 he bought Stainborough Hall expressly to create an estate suitable for a man of his importance, rather like I did when I had my conservatory done, and Queen Anne recreated the Earldom of Strafford and Thomas became the first Earl. I can't help thinking that they saw themselves as human chess pieces in some drawing-room game. Not pawns, obviously.

The Earl extended Stainborough Hall and, just because he could and because Wentworth Woodhouse had a suite of follies, built a mock medieval castle at the highest point of the estate, one of the first of a rash of such toff-follies built around that time. He called it Stainborough Castle and renamed the house Wentworth Castle, at a stroke creating a kind of faux-history that shone like fool's gold. Like a latter-day lottery winner or Premiership footballer, he built it for his children to play on, and each of the four towers was named after one of them. They were all painted a different colour inside, too, for Harriet, William, Lucy and Anne. Sadly, mining subsidence weakened much of the castle's structure, including two of the four towers, but recent restoration work has preserved much of the building for people like me and the Accrington Rat to wander around, once you've negotiated the ha-has.

There's a mock-Corinthian temple in the garden, built in the 1760s and commanding a view over the parkland because, as one blogger wrote, the Earl 'dotted the horizon with a virtual urban landscape of towers, mock fortifications, sham ruins and even a pyramid! Unhappily virtually all these works have completely disappeared, swallowed up by the urban sprawl of nearby Barnsley.' Other survivors include the obelisk called the Sun Monument, dedicated to Lady Mary Wortley Montague, which was said to have had a gleaming bronze disc on top of a spike protruding from the top of the structure that could be seen for miles around, hence the local name for the obelisk. In a different direction around the park you can find the Archers Hill Gate, a gate with three entrances that frame the landscape like that rectangle on a stick that Wordsworth used to carry around with him. There's a gun room, built in the nineteenth century when there was shooting on the estate, and a fake church by the entrance to the park called Steeple Lodge, which is now a private house. Further into the park, there's a Rotunda built to look like the Temple of Hercules near Rome and as the blogger Jim Jarrett points out 'it is worth remembering that if a folly has any purpose at all it is to be seen, to catch the eye. More often than not the building is but a featured component part of a greater overall plan, involving parkland, landscaping and ornamental features. The view is everything. Here at Wentworth Castle, where the park is now given over to agriculture and the Worsbrough ridge to urbanisation, much of that vision has gone forever. Happily for the Rotunda, the encroaching trees here have been felled and the old line of sight from the house re-established to restore the folly's original purpose.' Beyond the Rotunda there are two more obelisks and columns, the Queen Anne Column, built in 1734, and the Duke of Argyll Monument. By this time the casual visitor may be forgiven for admitting to folly fatigue, but it's worth remembering that it's truly remarkable to see all these rich men's toys in one place. A more recent extravaganza is the amazing nineteenth-century greenhouse which has been recently restored and licenced for weddings; actually, to call it a 'greenhouse' is not to do it justice. It's a conservatory that was built over 1885 and 1886 by the Essex-based firm of Crompton and Fawkes, and it's the only surviving example of their work today[17].

All this over-the-topness was designed to impress the people across the way at Wentworth Woodhouse, and a visit to Wentworth Castle illuminates this forgotten rivalry. Sadly some of the follies, like the Pavilion at the edge of the river and the pyramid known locally as the Smoothing Iron, have disappeared. By the 1980s, when I ran my writing workshops in the bar, the whole estate and the gardens were falling into disrepair[18] but thanks to a huge grant from the Lottery the area has been brought back to something like its former glory although sadly the gardens have gone into administration and have been closed to the public with the loss of a number of jobs and the possibility that the outside area will sink back into the undergrowth. Part of the problem has always been the split between the college and the grounds, and that's probably a problem to which there's no long-term solution; two visions of the world bump into each other with the idea of free adult education for all banging against the restoration of formal and eccentric parks and gardens into a local and national tourist attraction. I'd like to ask the Accrington Rat what he thinks might happen to the place in the long term but I've heard that, like the Smoothing Iron, he's no longer with us.

OXSPRING INGBIRCHWORTH

When I was a student at North Staffordshire Polytechnic in the 1970s I used to come home at weekends to work in Ernest Wiley's factory next to the Church Hall in Darfield. I partly came home to earn a few quid but I mainly came home to wallow in the sound of people talking like me. My first moments in Barnsley bus station were like that sequence in the 1939 film of *The Wizard of Oz* when Dorothy arrives in the land of Oz and the screen transforms from black and white to colour; the local lingo wrapped itself around me like a warm blanket. Then, on the Sunday night or first thing on the Monday morning, I'd catch a bus to Manchester, and then a train to Stafford, feeling the fizz of the language flattening as I drove away from the mothership. Looking back now I find it odd that I didn't get a train to Manchester but if I had I'd have missed out on Oxspring, a tiny village that the bus rumbled by.

Oxspring is on the edge of Barnsley as it crumbles into Sheffield and its position on the A629 has always meant that people pass though and say things like 'It would be nice to live here, wouldn't it?' and indeed it is, although the main road both connects and disturbs. As a young man on holiday from the Poly, which was most of the year as I recall, I once called into the Waggon and Horses with some of my mates and I recall that people stared at my pumps which were decorated with the Stars and Stripes. They stared so hard that the footwear almost spontaneously combusted. The same pumps had got me barred entry from a pub in Barnsley the night before; the bouncer had said 'Them sneakers are too much for this place', which was a polite way of telling me to get out. These days the Waggon and Horses is a wonderfully welcoming place; mind you, I don't wear Stars and Stripes pumps any more. Oxspring is a two-pub place and, like me and the lads all those years ago, people often drive out and sit in wooden chairs and drink beer that glints in the afternoon sun apart from the designated driver who drinks pop and burps quietly in the afternoon breeze.

Ingbirchworth is a village that's dominated by water, except in hot summers when people tell each other, as they mop their brows with their flat caps, that there isn't any water. There are three reservoirs around Ingbirchworth: Royd Moor, Scout Dike and Ingbirchworth itself, like a representation in land sculpture of the Three Wise Men. Get your stout shoes on and stroll round Ingbirchworth Reservoir; from above, on a map, it looks like an unfinished glove puppet and as you walk around it you feel like you're miles away from the throb and hum of Barnsley and Sheffield. From Ingbirchworth, now that you're a few inches higher from walking through all that mud, you should make your way to Royd Moor and Scout Dike reservoirs. Scout Dike reflects the sun on a summer's day and as it does so I see my dad and his mate Jack Greensmith, both trying flies they've made themselves. Some names in this area ring with a kind of linguistic significance for me; they're single words or pairs of sounds that become like poems. Great Houghton, because of my family connections, Dunford Bridge, because it sounds as remote as it is, and Scout Dike because my dad loved it so much, and just saying the words would make him happy.

My dad would stand by the water at Scout Dike in a battered hat and a coat that looked like it had fallen onto him from a crop-spraying plane. He would have a fishing fly in his mouth ready to pop it on a hook. Jack Greensmith would be attempting to light his pipe in a gale that sounded like a child's first bagpipe lesson. His concentrating brow would furrow to match the contours of the surrounding moors. My dad would raise his thumb to the sky and shout 'Better than work!' Jack would have liked to nod but he didn't want to spill his tobacco. When I accompanied my dad and Jack Greensmith and my Uncle Jack from Sheffield, who often called my dad (who was called John) Jack, it was like being out with a Beckettian Theatre Group called The Three Jacks. Uncle Jack would crack a raw egg into a Sheffield Wednesday cup and whip it up with a fork and then drink it. 'I was gagging for a raw egg in the Western Desert,' he would say. My dad would offer him a Mint Imperial.

The words Scout and Dike in that order also struck joy or fear into generations of Barnsley children as it was the outdoor centre that they went to at least once in their careers to learn to abseil or yomp or make fires by rubbing two teachers together. A week at Scout Dike was a necessary rite of passage for young people from Darfield or Darton or Thurnscoe; the centre was built in the 1960s and owned by the council and it's fair to say that it wasn't the Ritz. There was something about the Spartan nature of the place that people loved, however, and I've talked to many children (and teachers too) who remember the late night walks under the stars and the ghost stories by candlelight. For a while in the early years of this century the place was threatened with closure but it's flourishing now under new owners. My eldest daughter, a teacher, abseiled there with her pupils and I can report that the Scout Dike experience, now called the Kingswood experience, is alive and well. I didn't ask her about the ghost.

There's something seductive about these fringes of a town; they're fantastic places of escape and their car parks and pubs and cafés and benches are almost always full. Borders are exciting, and although the landscape doesn't change that much between, say, Barnsley and Kirklees or Barnsley and Doncaster, I always get a thrill from walking along a boundary. It feels like part of an ancient ritual, often accompanied by ice cream.

I'm pleased to announce, then, that there's a Barnsley Boundary Walk that doesn't quite fit the North/South/East/West/Central template of this book, but which is well worth trying to make your way around.

BORDER COUNTRY

As you come back home on the A628 from Manchester Airport with your duty free and your Trump-tan you pass through Hollingworth and Tintwistle and Crowden and you ascend a long hill and suddenly a sign tells you that you're in Barnsley. You look around for pitheads and glassworks but all you can see are vast empty spaces that look just like the vast empty spaces you were passing through before, while you were still in Tameside or Derbyshire. And yet you're in Barnsley, and there are two tiny settlements that are part of Pennine Barnsley and which are well worth a visit. I'm talking about Dunford Bridge and Townhead. Here's a tip: visit them in spring or summer, unless you're planning a long stay.

Dunford Bridge is now just a scattering of houses but once it was an important trans-Pennine site; there was a station there that served the line from Manchester to Sheffield as part of the Manchester-Sheffield-Lincoln Railway that survived until 1970 when the recently-electrified line was closed to passengers although the line was still there until the mid-1980s.[19] Stout-thewed and clear-eyed types flock to Winscar Reservoir, a hotbed (if that's the right term) of watersports and bird watching. There was a pub at Dunford Bridge, the Stanhope Arms, which closed down a few years ago and which at various times has almost become a hostel or a private house but somehow you get the sense that the past won't

let it; there's an almost crushing sense of history here, a feeling that the Industrial Revolution and the trains it needed to shift its goods are looking over your shoulder.

Near Dunford Bridge is Townhead, a couple of rows of terraced houses that, when I was a young man, was known as a hippy commune, where, to quote a taxi driver who once took me to the airport, 'Ivverybody is allus shagging on an eeap', a visual image which, once imagined, is hard to unimagine. There's still an experiment in communal living going on there but I don't know if the taxi driver's description still applies.[20]

A Deep Tarn Calendar – July

Got some shoooorts
An this: look. Just look
At this bugger.
Tha reyt: like a full mooin.
Else a flat snowball.
Else a coyne, a parnd coyne
Painted wi immulshun.
White flat cap: that tells thi
Its summer. Nowt tells thi
It's summer like one er theez.

A Deep Tarn Calendar – August

Reyt. Stand theer. Theer. Just
To thi left a bit. That's reyt. Theer.
Look up: look up at't sky
Can tha see it? A hint.
Nowt moor nor a hint
On Autumn. Semmas a crinkling
Rarnd edge on't sky.
A loss er clarity. A note
From't leet that sez
It's not allared ter play art
Cos it's delicutt.

A Deep Tarn Calendar – September

Thaz got thi ruler, thi new ruler
I'thi bag. Fust day. Fust day back.
New ruler. Ar. Fust day back at schooil.

Well mezzyer this: that long cowd rooad
Ter Christmas. Is thi new ruler long enuff?

Ar ooap sooah.

Notes

1. Pear Day, at the end of September, is an annual pear-based jamboree that takes over Cannon Hall with a celebration of all things pear. Perhaps the thinking was that if Wakefield can have a rhubarb festival then Cannon Hall can have a pear day. And why not, indeed? Perry good. Go to www.cannon-hall.com to find out more.

2. An early precursor of this tourism initiative was an advertising campaign that I vaguely remember from the 1960s called 'Barnsley, the Natural Centre of Attraction' which featured an image of a bowler-hatted bloke with an umbrella and a briefcase making his way across a map of the British Isles to Barnsley, which appeared to be closer to the middle of the country than it actually is.

3. The Jubilee Museum doesn't have a website as such but if you go on the www.visitpenistone.co.uk website you'll be able to find some details. Mind you, even the Visit Penistone website describes the museum as 'a typical Victorian hotch potch' and says, affectionately, that 'we wouldn't have it any other way.'

4. Cawthorne's other great attraction, of course is the folk singer Kate Rusby; Cawthorne's folk festival Underneath The Stars is very much a family affair. See www.underthe starsfest.com

5. For more information on the Waggonway, and to be guided along the train, visit www. visitpenistone.co.uk

6. The Penistone Line is run by Northern Rail and it really is a hidden gem of a line. The station names are like a poem in themselves: Denby Dale, Shepley, Honley, Brockholes, Stocksmoor, Berry Brow, Lockwood. The Penistone Line Partnership keep an eye on the line and fill it with activities: contact them at South Pennine Rail.co.uk

7. Somebody, (ok, me, in a Radio 4 programme) once said that Huddersfield was the Capital of Poetry and to a large extent that's still true. There's poetry, prose, song and storytelling all over the town and the Huddersfield Literature Festival does a great job of bringing national and international words to the place. www.litfest.org.uk

8. Penistone Paramount has its own website: www.penistoneparamount.co.uk

9. It's not strictly relevant to this book but Kevin Grunhill really is one of the leading cinema and theatre organists in the country and has played in all the top venues including the Tower Ballroom in Blackpool, so we should be especially proud that he's associated with Penistone. He's one of our own, as they say.

10. Harry Tufnell's goal has made him a legend in the town. He played for Barnsley between 1909 and 1920. When Barnsley got to the semi-final of the FA Cup in 2008 I wrote a

poem called 'Harry Tufnell's Booit' which I had to perform live on Radio 5 Live in The Full House pub in Monk Bretton in the company of a lot of excited and excitable reds fans, but I have to say their joining in on the refrain 'Harry Tufnell's booit!' was exemplary and oddly moving.

11. For a history of wire-drawing, there's a book by Michael Notis called *The History and Evolution of Wiredrawing*, available from googlebooks.

12. The Thurgoland Parish website is an invaluable resource: www.thurgoland.org.uk

13. Penistone Church is on Facebook, and they have information on this remarkable church.

14. There's very little information to be found about Saunderson, so the best thing to do is go and see the musical. Get details of when it might be performed again at www.no horizonthemusical.com or suggest a private performance in your house.

15. Have a look at the Northern College website: it'll give you a range of the things that go on there. It's a really inspiring place. www.wentworthcastle.org will fill you in on the history and the toff-rivalry.

16. Brian Sefton always told me he'd written a novel called *The Travelling Lamp* but I couldn't find it anywhere and in the end I worked out that it must have been unpublished. One day somebody, maybe me, will put out a book of his poems and stories.

17. Folk musician and explorer Jim Jarrett has written about the Wentworth Castle follies on his website www.jimjarrett.co.uk

18. There's lots about Wentworth Castle on the Parks and Gardens website www.parksand gardens.co.uk

19. There's a fantastic picture of Dunford Bridge station on www.disusedstations.org.uk, a magnificent site if you're looking for lost and forgotten platforms. It's a site that's very easy to get totally lost in, I have to warn you.

20. Last time I looked there was a wholefood delivery service operating out of Townhead, carrying on the hippy tradition without the heaps.

NORTH

CUDWORTH AND GRIMETHORPE

These days you can zoom to Grimethorpe down the new road that follows the route of the old railway line past the former Houghton Main and Grimethorpe pits, but years ago if you were going to Grimethorpe from Darfield you had to go down Edderthorpe Lane and through Cudworth. My Uncle Charlie once told me about a place called Longbottles between Darfield and Cudworth and to be honest, I thought he'd made it up, but on the *Gazetteer of England and Wales* there is a place called Long Bottles, but sadly the words are all I can find.

Grimethorpe and Cudworth are archetypal and exemplary Barnsley names. Everyone has heard of Grimethorpe because of the colliery band and *Brassed Off*. Cudworth is in the spotlight because of Michael Parkinson and because, if you're not from Round Here, it's a test of your pronunciation skills, on the same level as Dodworth but not with same difficulty rating as Barugh Green. We'll come to Penistone later, of course. Depending how good you are at pronouncing Cudworth.

Edderthorpe Lane winds and twists and crosses an old pit railway line and a deep wood called Storrs Mill Wood. If I venture into the wood I come across lots of fly-tipping, an old packhorse bridge and a number of faces carved into rock formations. There was a Storrs Mill, only the foundations of which remain, but it's well worth looking for because even if you don't find it, in spring you'll be walking through millions of bluebells.

I carry on down into Cudworth at the point that Edderthorpe Lane becomes Darfield Road. Michael Parkinson is not the only famous denizen of Cudworth, of course. There's Dorothy Hyman, the athlete who won silver and bronze medals at the 1960 and 1964 Olympics and after whom the Dorothy Hyman stadium in Cudworth and, confusingly for a short time, the Dorothy Hyman stadium in Wombwell were named and who won the 1963 Sports Personality of the Year, a pub quiz answer you can often thrash Southern softies with. There's a quiet pride in Dorothy Hyman in Cudworth and in the wider borough, because we like to see our own sons and daughters doing well on the national and international stage, and we like it when they stay round here and don't get dragged off to the bright lights of Rotherham. Cudworth's other Olympic medallist is Archibald Stinchcombe, who won gold in the unlikely, for this part of the world, discipline of ice hockey at the 1936 games. It must be something in the Cudworth air. Cudworth is also the home of the Cudworth pointillist, Mick Wilson, a marvellous artist who has been dotting the i's more than he's been crossing the t's for years. I think Mick should be better known than he is and maybe, just maybe, if he hadn't remained loyal to this part of the world he might have been.

Cudworth always reminds me of Wombwell in that it is a separate township of its own with a busy main street and a very distinct identity, not a suburb of Barnsley and not really a tiny village. It's that unusual thing, a pit settlement that never had a pit, with most of the mineworkers from Cudworth going to Grimethorpe or Houghton Main or into the pits nearer the town. It had a station until 1968, and indeed when the station was first opened in 1840 it was called Barnsley station, and there were helpful indications on the timetable that you could catch an omnibus into town from outside the station. It was renamed as Cudworth For Barnsley in 1854, which is like Alnmouth in Northumberland being called Alnmouth for Alnwick; as far as language is concerned, it's true, but as far as getting a bus or a taxi or hiring a car or walking goes, it's easier said than done.

One of the glories of Cudworth is its park, a proper green slice of municipal pride of the kind that were created in all these villages as places for miners to rest and recuperate and get a bit of sun on their backs; in my role as minor local celeb (Michael Parkinson must have been busy) I was invited to open the Cudworth Gala in the summer of 2016. I was happy to accept but the invitation opened up the old running sore of the Garla/Gayla conundrum, which is similar to the East Lothian Question or the Diet of Worms in its complexity. When I was young the annual Darfield Gala was the pinnacle of my social season, once you'd got the church garden party out of the way but it was a Gayla. In Cudworth I was invited to open a Garla. If I'd have been less of a man of the world I would have assumed that they were two different species of events, with one involving communities getting together to celebrate themselves and their place in the world and the other being a solitary chess game against a steam-driven machine. I joined the parade through the park, led by the twirling batons of the majorettes. The parade was a little late setting off because we had to wait for the vintage army vehicles. As a member of the crowd said, 'Good job they're not on their way to a bloody war.' I read out my poem of opening, managing to avoid saying either Garla or Gayla and was rewarded with a splendid signed football from the mighty Barnsley F.C.. I was then taken to the bowling green in the park which has fallen into disuse but has been reimagined as a Peace Garden, a moving and timely memorial to the men of Cudworth who died in the First World War with a mural in the old pavilion and a list of the fallen on the wall. I went back to the Gala (pronounce it how you want) and spent too much money on the tombola, getting lots of zeros or fives on my tickets and coming away with a wine glass, three bars of chocolate, a hairnet and some bath foam. Result.

Grimethorpe resonates in the popular imagination for various reasons but mainly because of, as I've hinted earlier, the Grimethorpe Colliery Band and the film *Brassed Off*. They seem to exemplify a nobility of struggle, a way of life built around work and art, a sense that even though you're far from the perceived centre of things, you can still lead a fulfilling cultural life. The band itself still practises in the Acorn Centre, a community building created in the wake of the closure of the pit, a closure that hit Grimethorpe particularly hard. Grimethorpe is an ancient settlement that, once the pit was sunk, was built around the colliery with two estates of houses known as White City and Red City, said to be because of the colours of the houses or the roofs. I remember a wag (in the old, rather than the new sense of the word) on a bus once saying 'There's three bits of Grimey: White City, Red City and Dodge City because they dodge behind't settee when't rent man comes.' The pit was one of the deepest in the country and at the time of its closure in 1993 it employed 6000 people.

Older Grimethorpe can still be glimpsed in West Haigh Woods, where I used to wander from the Great Houghton end on a Sunday afternoon. The Dell, a nature reserve that's often well stocked with fishermen, and the enigmatic Grimethorpe Hall, built in 1670 for Robert Seaton and his family. At the time Grimethorpe Hall was built, the village would have been a tiny scattering of farmsteads which grew rapidly with the arrival of the pit in 1896. Ferrymoor Pit, a deep drift mine, joined it in 1915. Over the years the Hall has become neglected and putative attempts to turn it into a pub have failed. Any restoration attempts have been put on hold because of a dispute over the ownership of the building; whenever I pass Grimethorpe Hall I'm amazed that it survives and I'm glad that it does because to me it exemplifies the way that history, with broken windows and a leaking roof, can stand amongst us to remind us that nothing is permanent. It's enough to make you want to dodge behind the settee.[46]

St Luke's Church has been called the Red Brick Cathedral, and it's a building that dominates the corner by Asda; if it's open, it's well worth sticking your head round the door. It was built in 1904 on land donated by Mr George Savile Foljambe (I just enjoyed writing the name down) and the interior is open and spacious and will certainly hold the last note of the Last Post for as long as it takes the congregation to file out.

There are a few clubs and pubs in Grimethorpe including the wonderfully named Bullet Club and the Red Rum pub. There was a pub, now demolished, called the Manor, and local man Dick Bateman writes in a walking guide 'Going back to the fifties, the Manor had its own band all dressed in red blazers and red ties. And it had waiter service! Unbelievable in a village like this for a pub to have waiter service and its own band. Those were good times.' I believe the good times are on their way back to Grimethorpe, and maybe one day the Bullet Club will have its own band in red blazers and waiter service.

BRIERLEY

Brierley is another one of those Barnsley villages that is on the cusp of West Yorkshire; it's only two miles to Hemsworth and for a lot of the citizens to go to town is to go to Hemsworth rather than into Barnsley.

It's also, though not to the extent of Dodworth, Cudworth and Barugh Green, a pronunciation trap that many, including me, have fallen into over the years. You see, not being from there, I say the name of the village Breerley to rhyme with beer, but the inhabitants of the place refer to it as Bryerley, to rhyme with pie. If you turn up with your beer and they're expecting pie, then they know you're a stranger in town and all the talk in the saloon (there isn't a saloon) will stop and people will turn and look at you 'gone out' as they say round here.

Like many places in the borough, it's an ancient one, with evidence of early Saxon settlements and, between Brierley and Grimethorpe, a lost manor house called Hall Steads and an existing hall called Folly Hall, which is now a farm just off the road to Hemsworth. Intriguingly, on Brierley Common there's the site of an old oak tree called Old Adam which was the last of a small wood called the Well-Bred Oaks. The History of Brierley website is very matter of fact about the demise of Old Adam: 'The tree became a dead trunk in the twenties and had gone by 1930.' It'll happen to all of us, I suppose.

The Brierley Village website is a labour of love and a model for how this kind of endeavour can be broadcast to a wider public. Again and again I become aware of my ignorance of the places that aren't too far away from where I'm typing this and as well as strolling around a place, the virtual strolling around a good local history website can fill in the gaps. On the website I found the story of the Court Leet of Brierley, an ancient tradition that was still happening in the 1960s when Stan Bristow, a reporter for the *South Yorkshire Times*, attended one of these venerable events in the Three Horseshoes. I'll let him take up the story:

'As I entered, a bailiff was just calling 'Oyez Oyez! All manner of persons that have anything to do at the Court Leet here about to be holden for the Manor of Brierley, draw nigh and give your attendance, and ye shall be heard!' Bristow describes an anachronistic but utterly fascinating ritual. 'The duties of the Brierley Court Leet are now reduced to caring for the local commons upon which, according to the deeds of his property, each member has the right to graze so many cattle, or geese, or donkeys… Generally, the atmosphere of the meetings of the Court Leet is cordial although several of the common lands have been let for farming, a development of the last war when every acre of land put under food cultivation was valuable, a little acrimony has crept in with regard to what happens to the revenue from the leasing of the land… there is a school of thought that the court members (who are known as commoners, by the way) having lost some of their gazing rights, should receive some of the income by way of compensation.' Arthur Hargreaves, a farmer from Shafton, suggests 'that the revenue be used to provide the commoners with the same 'goodly feast' that used to mark the closure of the court. Arthur has been a member long enough to have personal recollection of the feasts, with tables groaning with a baron of beef and plenty of whisky and rum…and takes a poor view of the pickles and sandwiches that are now dispersed.' The Court Leet has disappeared from the Three Horseshoes and from the consciousness of the people of Brierley, but it bubbles just below the surface, as all the history of this place does. Maybe somebody, somewhere, perhaps in an elderly persons' lunch club, will use a phrase like 'I'll tek thi to't Court Leet if tha dun't gimme that money tha owes me!'

I'm interested in the use of the word 'feast' in this context; in Barnsley it's often, amongst the older generation, used to mean what other people in less heavenly parts of the country would call a fair. 'The feast is coming' we would say to each other as children, and we'd pronounce it in the Barnsley way: 'feeast.' Tuby's, the local funfair operators, will still put posters up advertising Darfield Feast or Wombwell Feast, and the traditional pit holiday in Barnsley, the second week in August, is still known as Barnsley Feast Week, with the week two weeks before that (because you got paid in hand) known as Bull Week because you worked like a bull, taking all the overtime you could, to give you enough money in your pocket to splash about at feast week. From the bull to the feast in a few short days.

It's all a matter of weeks and weekends in a village like Brierley and a town like Barnsley. When I was younger a lot of people got paid on Thursday so the pubs and clubs were full to bursting. The weekend would begin on Friday, when people rushed into the pub as though they thought it might be demolished if they didn't get to the bar quickly enough. Saturday was known as 'couples' night' when the mester and the lass went and sat on small tables and watched a turn. The practice of asking a woman if she wants a lady's glass for her half pint has almost died out, but not quite; it still persists, I'm told, in certain brightly lit drinking dens. Sunday dinnertime was when men would go to the pub or the club and then go home, eat a massive dinner and then fall asleep, snoring like dolphins. This is, of course, old fashioned and it comes from a time of hard physical graft down a red-hot pit and the need to slake the thirst and eat from plates the size of bin lids, but it still persists in the 24/7 gig economy, oddly. Taxi drivers, who know these things, tell me that the weekend has shrunk to Saturday night, and later on Saturday night as people pre-load. Payday weekend can sometimes stretch to Friday, but the town as a whole is still waiting and will be whenever this book is published and whenever you're reading it, for an economic miracle to replace the well-paid skilled jobs that were screwed up and thrown in the bin in the 1980s. Mind you, parts of Barnsley are still either Neanderthal or traditional, depending on your point of view. The practice of men calling women 'our lass' still persists, and you also occasionally hear the locution 'our Gert', an unfathomable (to me, anyway) phrase. I once read an interview with someone from Sheffield (outside the scope of this book and therefore of no interest to us) in the *Guardian* and the southern reporter wrote about a bin-man and his wife Gertrude. That'll be our Gert then.

The Industrial Revolution brought the usual changes to Brierley. The main pit in the village, apart from some smaller ones that had briefly flourished in the nineteenth century, was Brierley Colliery which worked from 1910 to 1947. It was partially owned by Captain Addy, of the Carlton Main Colliery Company, who also built Brierley Hall. After the closure, ironically just before nationalisation, many of the men in the village worked at Grimethorpe or some of the mines in West Yorkshire; like most of the villages in Barnsley, Brierley still feels like it maintains its links with the past, as though the pre-industrial times are still there, just sleeping, waiting for the noise of the gig economy to wake them up.

Brierley was my destination most Sunday mornings for a few years when I went to watch my grandson play football for the Brierley Cubs on Brierley Park; my route would take through Darfield, down the new bypass that has opened Grimethorpe up to the world, up the hill and into Brierley. Not far from the football ground is a fascinating old building called Lindley House, parts of which date back to the eighteenth century; of course there's a ghost, as noted in a fascinatingly written article from the ShellMex and BP

Group magazine of June 1969: 'Roy Schofield, Shell retail sales representative for Doncaster, and his attractive wife May' (I know: well, it was 1969) 'believe in ghosts. They live in Lindley House in the village of Brierley, reputedly haunted by the ghost of a footman'. So far so scary. However: 'Neither Roy nor May have actually seen the spectre, but May is sure one day she will.' That's okay then. Later in the piece the writer mentions that during the First World War the house was used as a convalescent home for wounded army officers and the matron, (it doesn't say if she was attractive) 'ran out in her night attire having been disturbed by strange sounds'. Well, we all would. The sounds of the football on Brierley Park would scare anybody to death and cause them run out in their night attire, especially when the Cubs score.

Just as it would be unusual to have two halls in Kensington called the Albert Hall, it's unusual that there are two churches very close to each other in Brierley and Grimethorpe called St Paul's, although to be strictly accurate one is called St Paul's and one is called The Anglican Church of St Paul, with no apostrophe and no S.

The Anglican church in Brierley was almost, like many of these nineteenth-century churches, a vanity project, being built in 1869 for George Savile Foljambe, the lord of the manor, in the gothic revival style. It was actually a chapel of ease for the much older church at Felkirk, just over the border in West Yorkshire. The church is well worth a visit and has been restored and cared for by the Friends of St Paul.

Brierley Hall was, after nationalisation, bought by Hemsworth Rural District Council and used as council offices; it was taken over by Barnsley Council in 1972. They kept the modern extension on the side which had been built in the 1960s by the Rural Council and the people of the village rejoiced when it was demolished in 2009. The Hall itself is now part of a development of new houses, or as the developer's advert has it, 'dwellings'. Colonel Addy would revolve in his grave. Or maybe not: he liked to see the place doing well.

ROYSTON

Maybe I should have put Royston into the 'language' section of this book because the way they talk, or are perceived to talk, or used to talk, is one of the defining characteristics of the people of this village on the edge of Barnsley, almost on the cusp of West Yorkshire.

The linguist Kate Burland has made an extensive study of the dialect(s) of Royston and her findings reveal coalbucketloads of information about the way that this part of the world has always been a melting pot of people coming here to find work.

Royston is in many ways a typical village of the sort that this book is made up of. It was a farming village but during the industrial revolution it expanded hugely thanks to the arrival of the canal and the railway and the coalmines. Monckton Main opened in 1878 and closed in 1966, and Royston Drift Mine opened almost a hundred years later and lasted a little while after the strike, closing in 1989. The main visual marker of Royston for many years was the Monckton Coking Plant with its distinctive chimneys that could be seen from miles around, often puthering smoke into the air, a sign to many Roystoners getting back from holiday that they were coming home. After being operative for more than 130 years it finally closed in December 2014; a union official said at the time that it was 'the final nail in the coffin of the coal industry in South Yorkshire' and he was right. There was also, as there often was in these villages, a factory providing employment for the women while the men went to work; in this case the Valusta factory which made shirts from the 1940s to the 1980s. It's significant to me that the shirt factory closed in the 1980s; the toy factory in Darfield closed in 1984 and so much of the town's urban and industrial infrastructure was coming to halt in that decade that it still amazes and heartens me that the town had the courage and the strength to fight back and not lay down and die.

Again, like many of the Barnsley villages, Royston has a magnificent and ancient church, a thread of history that perhaps proves the pits and the canals and the railways will simply be a little wrinkle in the long rug of history. The church of St John the Baptist has a ring of eight bells, without Yorkshire Tail Ends, and was built in 1234; it's demi-semi-unique (a term I just coined) because it's one of only three churches in the country to have an oriel window, a kind of half-bay window that doesn't quite reach to the ground. In its time, Royston has had two railway stations, one called Notton and Royston and one called Royston and Notton, with the word 'and' being the fulcrum they both turn around. Notton and Royston opened in 1882 and closed in 1930 and Royston and Notton opened in 1841 and closed in 1968 so for a while it would have been possible to get a return from Notton and Royston and Royston and Notton.

As well as World Heritage Sites, celebrating significant architectural treasures old and new, grand and vernacular, UNESCO also run a scheme called Intangible Heritage which takes note of things like dances and songs and rituals and the French four course meal eaten at home. It's my view that the unique Royston dialect, or what's left of it in the changing linguistic air of the early twenty-first century, could become a piece of UNESCO intangible heritage.

Kate Burland's fascinating and stimulating research, which mainly dates from 2010, discusses the fact that a lot of people believe that there's only one Barnsley accent, which is of course untrue. I pride myself as being a bit of a local Henry Higgins and I bet I could guess which part of the borough people came from in three goes just by getting them to say a couple of key words like 'door' and 'school'. Dooer and Schooil would mark them out, in my (not scientific or academic in any way) estimation as coming from the south end of Barnsley whereas in the north end, towards the West Yorkshire border, they would say Dore, to sound like the village near Sheffield and Skewel to sound like fuel. Okay, maybe I'm Henry Higgins's less intellectual brother Cyril.

Kate Burland writes that Royston was known as 'Little Staffordshire' and the inhabitants were called 'Staffies' because a number of people came to settle there from struggling pits and farms in Staffordshire in the nineteenth century; in the thirty years between 1871 and 1911 the population of the village increased nine times. Burland notes that the perceived variations in the dialect, as expressed by local people, could be because a lot of the incomers came from Staffordshire and the Black Country but it could also be because, as I've already noted, Royston is on the map-fold or the staple in the atlas right next to West Yorkshire, and there's possibly a South Yorks/West Yorks isogloss there. An isogloss is a linguistic term for changes in language that occur over a small geographical space; the most striking one I know of is the one I've written about so many times before that it's become known (by me, anyway, and then only in private) as McMillan's Isogloss or the house/arse interface, which occurs on the border of Sheffield and Chesterfield where the house becomes the arse, as in 'I've just had an extension built on my arse.'

Burland collects and reports the words of a local mineworker who says 'Monckton Main Coal Company continued to expand generating a "Klondyke" atmosphere drawing a number of young mineworkers from the "Black Country". Some like my own father came from Netherton near Dudley in 1897, aged seventeen, he along with several workmates walked the 110 miles to Royston.' As far as I can see from the research and from my very limited knowledge of linguistics the differences hinge around the word 'goat' and the word 'face', about the way the vowels and consonants crash and bump against each other like dodgems at a fair. I suggest you buy a dog called GoatFace and walk it round Royston and see if you can become part of this ongoing study. Then drop a line to UNESCO.

BARUGH GREEN

I'm not angling for more voice-over work but the proper way to consume *Real Barnsley* would be as an audiobook; the language of a place is its architect's plan and its building blocks, its footings and its roof trusses. This borough talks to itself and to the world in a dialect that is beautiful and musical and which sings with words for ways of working that have all but disappeared. To listen to someone from Barnsley speaking is to listen to all the Barnsley speakers there have ever been; you can almost glimpse all those shadowy people listening and nodding or shaking their heads. If an actor tries to portray someone from Barnsley there are several linguistic traps, well-laid and covered, for the unwary.

The name of the village of Barugh Green on the northern edge of town is the apex of Barnsley pronunciation tests. It's the pinnacle. It's the Daddy. It's the maze in which many people find themselves lost, sometimes forever. You can occasionally see them waving from the far end of the main street on a moonlit night.

Of course outsiders (which includes most people, let's be honest) struggle with Cudworth and Dodworth, calling them Cudworth and Dodworth rather than Cudeth and Dodeth, and there are lingo-traps set around Great Houghton and Little Houghton because of the odd and unique way we say the Houghton word round here, but Barugh Green leaves unwary visitors word-stranded and gasping for air. Let me help you out here: it's not Baroog Green. It's not Baroof Green. It's not Barf Green. It's Bark Green, like the noise a dog might make or what a tree is covered in.

Barugh Green, like most of the villages around Barnsley, was rural until the Industrial Revolution. The name derives from the old word 'berg' which meant 'hill'. And there's evidence that people, pronouncing the word correctly or not, were settling in the area from Anglo-Saxon times. Years ago, there was a parish of Barugh that included the nearby areas of Higham (the cricket ground behind the Engineers Arms is a real gem, especially when the sun goes down and somebody scores a magnificent six), Gawber and Pogmoor and as you walk down Barugh Green's main street I think you can still get just a whiff of the pre-industrial layout. There was a sixteenth-century Manor house which no longer exists, and a mill that was still in situ until 1968 when, amazingly, it was broken up and the mill wheel sent to York. I guess I shouldn't be amazed because the 1960s were the decade of breaking things up and getting new ones. I remember this as a time of Piano Smashing Competitions, and the joy we felt at being able to pass an old Joanna from a pub front room or a chapel back room through a toilet seat. The smashing up was bad enough, but the toilet seat was a clammy and shuddering indignity that acts as a metaphor or an emblem for much of the lost past of our towns and cities. The competitions began much earlier but they seemed to reach their peak in the year men landed on the moon, perhaps looking for a piano.

In the eighteenth century everything was new around this part of the world; the coal owners realised that they needed some method of mass transportation to get their black gold from A to B and so the Barnsley Canal was built nearby, gleaming like a knife through landscape. Pits were sunk and in the early twentieth century eighty coke ovens were built, staining the sky with the colour of labour and money, and at Barugh Coke Works they employed many people through the decades.

A few years ago I felt like I was being broken up and forced through a toilet seat of my own devising when I couldn't remember the name of the group I was meant to be delivering a talk to on a Monday afternoon in Barugh Green in early autumn. All I had in my diary was the word Green preceded by the word Barugh and a time: 13.30. Normally when I've got a local gig, one of the ones where they pay me in home-made chutney, I write down the name and number of the organiser but I must have been distracted (perhaps by news of a piano-smashing competition) so I didn't. But, of course, being distracted is no help when you're due to give a talk and you don't know where or who to.

In those days I wasn't on Twitter or Facebook, and indeed this may well have been pre-social media, and so in order to find out where the talk was, I did the most sensible thing I could: I wrote a column in the *Barnsley Chronicle* about it. At least the readers, unless they were off-comed 'uns, would know how to say the name of the place. My piece in the paper laid out my dilemma; I knew I was talking to someone somewhere in the village. I knew the day. I just didn't know where. A couple of hours after the paper hit the newsagents and got scuttled around the streets in the panniers of paper boys and girls, someone rang to tell me the address of the community centre where the event was happening, and that I was talking to the Barugh Green Local History Group at the centre on the main street.

Barugh Green, like many of the local villages, has been denuded of the pubs that used to slake the thirst of those who'd worked down the pit or in the coking plant; the Phoenix and the Spencer's Arms have gone, and the Working Men's Club carries on as best it can in a world that has forgotten the collectivism that gave birth to the club movement and thrived as the working population grew.

Where's that toilet seat?

DARTON

I first went to Darton many years ago because I woke up there. I'd been to a poetry gig in Sheffield and I'd had what people telling anecdotes to workmates in brightly lit offices call 'a couple of beers';

I'd tangoed onto the last train to Wombwell, knowing that I could trundle myself home from there on ale-wheels. I got into my seat and fell deeply asleep, snoring, dribbling and twitching at the same time in a rare three-pronged total eclipse of the brain. I slept past Attercliffe Road and Brightside stations. I slept past where Meadowhall station would be built in several years. I slept past Chapeltown and Elsecar. I slept, fatally, past Wombwell. I slept past Barnsley. I woke up with a shuddering gasp at Darton and staggered off down some unfamiliar streets, the A to Z in my head replaced by a tattered B to Y. The station was unmanned and had been since 1970, a hundred and twenty years after it first opened. Old photographs show a substantial station building with a booking office and a waiting room and a clutch of uniformed railway workers standing by a couple of passengers in posh shirts and ties, presumably worn for the photographer's benefit. So a few years earlier a kindly station manager, possibly with a big handlebar moustache, would have guided me to the other platform and the service back to Wombwell. So, unfairly, Darton has always been for me a nexus of misplacement, a place of being not quite where I thought I was or think I am.

Darton is, of course, blameless in all this. It's a village that rubs shoulders with the M1 motorway at Junction 38 and the distance to West Yorkshire can be measured in yards. Like so many of the villages around Barnsley, it has an ancient church around which the

settlement clusters, and which dominates the place as you pass, having missed your stop on the train. The church is described as 'one of the most complete and unaltered Late Perpendicular churches in South Yorkshire' and I took note of that decades ago when I sat on a tomb contemplating walking back to Darfield. If the church is open, have a look inside; light seems to be filtering through air that has been collected between the walls for hundreds of years. The light could come from, to use the muscular, rhythmic, poetic language of Pevsner, the 'moulded west doorway, 3-light west window. Tall, transomed 2-light bell-chamber openings... 3-light south aisle and south chapel windows with arched heads. Large 5-light transomed east window. 3-light north-aisle windows with depressed-arched lights and square heads. Similar 2-light clerestory windows whose hoodmoulds have figure-head stops in lighter coloured stone.'

There are six bells in the tower, and they've recently been refurbished; for completists I can tell you that they're in the key of G, and I have a vague memory of going to ring them once in the late 1970s which would have been about the same time I got off the train at the wrong stop. Ah, it's all coming together; Darton and I are subtly intertwined, somehow.

Like most of Barnsley's villages, as well as a church, Darton has a Big House, in this case Birthwaite Hall, once a single dwelling, now a listed building converted into a number of apartments. The

hall was built in the late eighteenth century by Thomas Rishworth, a banker originally from Hemsworth near Wakefield and who was very prominent in Wakefield society at the time until his bank collapsed and he returned to Hemsworth. Birthwaite Hall is beautiful, hidden from the A638 and yet another one of those places round here that makes you gasp and say 'Well! I never knew that was here!' Unless you live in Darton and you knew all along; place of mystery, you see, always mystery.

Many years after my 'wrong station' debacle I went to Darton with my wife to watch our grandson play football. The manager of the team often gave directions to the ground from the Philip Glass school of mapreading: a few words, repeated. 'You go down that hill and you turn just before the bend. Make sure you turn just before the bend. Make sure you turn just before that bend. Down the hill and turn just before the bend.' He then got into his car and zoomed off and so of course we got lost because we couldn't keep up with him. He was a milkman so you'd think he would have driven slowly and stopped frequently but that wasn't the case. In a perfect world we would have had a satnav in the car but we didn't and anyway we didn't know where the football ground in Darton was to key it into the satnav. In a less-than-perfect world my wife or I would have had our phones with us so that we could have found the ground fairly easily but for unfathomable reasons we'd left them at home.

I only write this personal episode in a topographical, historical and travel book to illustrate that my wife and I were simply illustrating the fact that for many years in Barnsley and towns like Barnsley, people never visited villages at the other end of the borough except, perhaps, for sporting or musical occasions. Or to ring bells and get off a train, in my case. Although Darfield and Darton share a first syllable there really was no reason for the general population of each village to know much about the other. This means that some places you know like the back of your hand and some places, only a few miles away, you know like the back of your neck, the bit the barber shows you when he's cut your hair, the bit you don't know very well. Making this book has transplanted lots of Barnsley from my neck to my hand. And anyway, watching children and grandchildren play sport or sing or dance is an almost Walter Benjaminesque way of getting to know a locality: amplifying place by the shape of goalposts or the rattle of tap shoes on a church hall floor.

My wife and I followed the vague instructions. We went down the hill and we turned just before the bend. I promise you we turned just before the bend. There was no sign of any kind of football match. We had ended up in front of the church. We asked a passing youth if he knew where the football field was. 'You could try the Long Fields' he said, pointing vaguely beyond the church tower. I thought I knew about the Long Fields because I'd seen them on a map of old Darton, near a pond called The Wash; they were a green lung for Darton, a place where people strolled and, hopefully, played football. I'd also seen the Long Fields more recently on a poster about a summer festival, The Coalfields Festival, so it certainly felt like the kind of place teams of Under 11s might be playing in a crunch match in the Charles Rice League.

We got to what we thought were the Long Fields but they turned out to be Darton Park, where kiddies were laughing because, as Brecht said, they hadn't heard the bad news. We asked a lad who could have been the brother of the first boy we asked about the whereabouts of the game. He pointed in the direction we came from 'Probably on the Long Fields' he said.

We walked back into the centre of town. My wife had an idea: 'Let's just stand still and listen', she said, 'and we'll be able to hear the match.' That was a plan. We stood and looked up, as though the sounds of shouting parents and small boots kicking big footballs might fall from the air like tiny sonic messages. We must have looked like people straining to catch the sound of a train leaving a tunnel miles away, so as to decide whether to run for it. In the distance we could hear wagons rumbling into the yard at Shaw Carpets to take floor-covering to the world. Like a number of people, I've always associated Darton with Shaw Carpets and their logo of a Native American Chief who appears to be sitting on a (presumably) Shaw Carpet and is now gazing into the distance beyond Woolley Edge Services. As a younger poet travelling the country doing gigs I was always cheered by the sight of the Shaw Carpets Native American rumbling down the motorway or parked on a high street, covering the nation with hard-wearing Barnsley produce.

As we stood I thought, as I've been thinking for months, about this book and the way that it could also be a soundscape as well as a series of Cheeveresque sentences on the page. You could include the clank of pit wheels and the rattle of trains, the shouting of market vendors and the running of deer across a huge park. You could include the harsh braying of the voices of the landed gentry, the stentorian shouts of the waistcoated self-made men and the multiple accents and dialects of the people who did all the work.

That evening, though, we couldn't hear any football match. Another young man who looked just like the first two (in fact he could have been the same person in a different hoodie) passed by and we asked him, even though we knew that the match must be over by now, if he had any idea where we might find a football game. He pointed to a row of shops and said 'It might be down there. That's where the cricket club is.' He pointed to what appeared to be two shops, then I noticed a path, a narrow path. My wife and I walked down it tentatively as though we were entering a wardrobe is a C.S. Lewis book.

We met my grandson and his team walking back; somehow the match had been down where the third of our guides pointed. And yet somehow the Cricket Club, as I found out later, was on the Long Fields. And yet I thought we'd been to the Long Fields earlier.

Ah, Darton, village of mystery.

DODWORTH AND GILROYD

This book is, of course, about real places, hence the name. But sometimes the unreal creeps into nomenclature via collective memory and ordinary streets take on an almost mythical glow and they sing with possibility even when nobody's listening. So, scattered across the paragraphs of these pages and the streets of this borough, there's Sodom, near Stairfoot Roundabout, and there's Bare Booans in town. There's Plevna at Little Houghton and Cat Hill in Darfield.

And at Dodworth, an old settlement that's now the kind of village advertised as being 'convenient for Junction 37 of the M1', there's the uber-mythical site 'The top of Dodworth Bottoms'. If you ask people where it is they will often say 'Near the bottom of Dodworth Tops' which means that they don't know. I'm not sure, either, but it's a good excuse for a stroll round Dodworth. The top of Dodworth Bottoms is either here. Or here.

One salient point about Dodworth is that, like Wombwell and Goldthorpe, it's been by-passed by a bypass. Years ago it was a kind of gateway to the A628, to the Woodhead Pass and Manchester Airport, and if you fancied a night out in Tintwistle, you'd drive through Dodworth and perhaps get ensnared by its charms and abandon Tintwistle's Latin Quarter one more time. Now the road snakes past Dodworth and makes its own way by the old pitstack of Dodworth Main Colliery which finally closed in 1987 when it was known as Redbrook, and out by the industrial units to the wide moors yonder.

Years ago I went to Dodworth to watch a rugby league match; it's odd that Barnsley is a kind of rugby league desert, a football and rugby union town surrounded by Wakefield Trinity Wildcats and Castleford Tigers and Featherstone, er, Rovers, but that's mainly due to the influence of the Reverend Tiverton Preedy who started Barnsley F.C. and who appears elsewhere in *Real Barnsley* telling anyone who'll listen that the round ball is better than the oval one. There have been the odd attempts to foster Rugby League in Barnsley though, and one of the more successful outings is Dodworth Rugby League Club, which in the 1990s and in the new millennium played in the Conference, a division of mainly smaller local teams from across the League heartlands of Yorkshire and Lancashire.

I remember that my trip to Dodworth to watch the rugby league began with a trip to Roland's Fisheries. The eponymous Roland was a scholar of fish and chips and indeed I once interviewed him on a local radio show about how to make the perfect mushy peas; he was a marvellous guest and so I invited him back to talk about batter. Then, in perhaps the wrong order but because it was on its way to the Welfare Ground, I called for a drink at what it now the Holiday Inn but which was then a hotel called Brooklands which was always reputed to be the best place in the area to eat that local delicacy the Barnsley Chop, and indeed was said by some to be the chop's birthplace.

Delicacy is perhaps the wrong word for the Barnsley Chop, which is traditionally a double chop, just enough to plug the hungry mouths of Barnsley men and stop them telling anecdotes about life down the pit for a few minutes. The origins of this gigantic cut of meat are, as I hinted earlier, a little obscure. Some say that the local (and much missed) butcher Albert Hurst prepared one for the visit of the Prince of Wales in 1933 when he came to open the brand new Town Hall. Others say that the first one was made at the Royal Hotel in the middle of town, and another faction insist that it first saw the light of oven at Brooklands. In the days when fine dining was a rarity round these parts Brooklands was the place to go if you wanted waiter service and a separate bloke in a dickie bow to pour the wine for you. Most people in Barnsley preferred simple fare and were wary of anything that smacked of pretension, so that when my wife and I, before we were married, went to the Co-op Restaurant and, after our dinner, to show how cutting-edge and *d'aujourd hui* I was, said to the waitress 'Could I have the cheese course please?' She looked at me like my mam did if I happened to say the word 'lunch' and said 'Certainly sir, red or white?'

So having had my chips at Roland's and my pint at Brooklands, I ventured to the Welfare Ground to watch some Rugby League. Dodworth Miners Welfare ground is a fantastic example of the welfare grounds that dot the borough; you'll find other good ones at Grimethorpe and Goldthorpe. These are part of the cradle-to-grave philosophy of the old NCB; they gloried in the idea of collectivism in sport and the idea that people who worked together should play together too. There are football fields and rugby fields and a small stand to shelter from the weather in. Access is gained, as it should be, by the side of the Miners Welfare Hall itself.

On the day I went to watch the rugby it was drizzling and this added to the drama of the game, as well as making sure that the little clutch of spectators got almost as muddy as the players. At my school we played Rugby Union, which I've always thought of as being inferior to league and just because I'm from the North, League seems faster somehow, because after five tackles something has to happen. Union can be slow and all the rucks and mauls and scrums make the game, especially at amateur level, resemble watching a sponge cake sink slowly and dramatically when it's taken out of the oven too soon.

In the game the Dodworth players looked like men and the opposition, who I think were from somewhere towards York, looked like boys. Indeed, I have a vivid recollection of a man turning to his mate and saying, 'It's men against boys.'

Dodworth Chronicle, a blog begun in 2009, and an authoritative view of matters historical in Dodworth, says that the area known as Dodworth Bottom has been called by that name since at least the seventeenth century, when it was said to have been given as a parcel of land by a wealthy landowner as a present to his daughter. Mind you, many of the entries in the *Dodworth Chronicle* end with the phrase 'Do you know anything about this?' which is of course the charming and knowledge-crowdfunding thing about blogs: they're journals of enquiry as much as journals of record. I might end each chapter of this book with the phrase 'Do you know anything about this?' because then we'll all come to understand that history is not a closed-off entity but an open book.

There is an ancient building in Dodworth, opposite the library; the date on it is 1641, but an older timber-framed house on the site dated from 1621, and it was built by a member of one of the wealthier families in Dodworth, the Brookes. He was a tanner from Huddersfield, and the family owned three tanyards, as they were called, in the village. Do you know anything about this?

Gilroyd is a village that is almost co-terminus with Dodworth, and again, like Dodworth and Cudworth and Barugh Green, is a degree-level pronunciation test. As an outsider from Darfield, I would say Gilroyd, with the emphasis on the first syllable. Gilroyders of my acquaintance would bang hard into the second syllable, calling it Gilroyd. It's both a small difference and a big difference at the same time. There's a delicate ecology between Dodworth and Gilroyd that's like that between Great Houghton and Little Houghton; one nods at the other, but won't shake its

hand, if I can be allowed to be a little poetic.

Back at the rugby league match at Dodworth, what I can recall of it is that it certainly was a match of boys against men, but the boys ended up winning because they were faster and fitter. They didn't seem to enjoy themselves as much as the men, though.

From the Welfare Ground I walk to Dodworth Station, a new station, opened in 1989 on the site of the previous station, which has been opened as part of the South Yorkshire Railway in 1854. It was rebuilt by the Manchester, Sheffield and Lincolnshire Railway towards the end of the nineteenth century, but closed to passenger traffic in 1959; coal trains used the line until the pit shut in 1987, but after two years of silence a (symbolic) whistle was heard again.

The new station is the epitome of the word 'functional', with a basic shelter, one platform, and a shelter that seems to invite wind and rain rather than repelling it. Years ago there was a station at Summer Lane which closed in 1959. Sadly, Disusedstations.co.uk can't help with a picture. You can still, thrillingly (well, for chaps like me) see the ghost platforms and I for one was a little disappointed when they didn't reopen that one as well. Mind you, there were a few houses in the way.

JUNCTION 38

Interestingly, Junction 38 on the M1 denies that it has anything to do with Barnsley at all; if you approach it from the North or the South it purports to be an exit for Huddersfield. Lots of people get off there to go to the Yorkshire Sculpture Park or the National Mining Museum both of which are not in Barnsley and therefore of no interest to us. It's true that Junction 38 is a kind of frontier post, a border crossing between South and West Yorkshire, between Barnsley and Kirklees.

Unlike Barnsley's other two M1 junctions, there's not much of an industrial hinterland here; there are no warehouses or units making small things very precisely. There's a pub, the Old Post Office, where you can get a steak as big as Rutland. Cross the roundabout at the junction and go into Woolley Colliery Village, which one source says is known locally as Mucky Woolley to distinguish it from the more affluent village of Woolley, a few miles away towards Wakefield.

The first time I went to Woolley Colliery Village I was in the company of some other writers from a group at the nearby Bretton Hall College led by poet and climber Terry Gifford; we'd decided to walk around the village and write (I shudder and blush as I recall this) Authentic Poetry About Authentic Places. Woolley Colliery was certainly authentic and we scuttled about with our notebooks like we were important. There were two main streets: Top Row and Low Row, and I vividly remember a green hut that was a fish and chip shop. A woman watched us from a doorway and said, loud enough for us all to hear 'I wish students had better things to do than act daft' to which Terry Gifford, with admirable aplomb, replied 'We're not acting daft, we're acting sensible'. She closed the door. There's a tiny war memorial in the village and the Wakefield Family History Sharing Group have made a detailed and touching record of the stories behind the names on their website. I wish such things had existed when I went on my poem-writing junket all those years ago; there's the poetically-named Aquilla Mitchell, who 'was the son of Thomas and Sarah Booth Mitchell, they lived at Top Row, Woolley Colliery with Aquilla, a servant and two boarders. Aquilla died of wounds on the 5th of June 1916.' There's Wilson Mitchell who 'enlisted in Barnsley, joining the York and Lancaster Regiment. He was killed in action on the first day of the Battle of the Somme.'

There's a lovely cricket ground at Woolley Colliery with a lovely pavilion from which, if you've got any sense, you can watch the match. My grandson played there in the first away match of the season one icicle April and my hands were so cold I couldn't clap when he made a catch.

The whole landscape of Woolley Colliery and the surrounding area has been changed by the arrival of Woolley Grange, a new housing estate that is almost a village of its own; there's an active resident's association, and splendid views across the motorway to the farmland and Emley Moor mast. The estate mirrors the streets and rows that sprang up when the pits came and shows that Barnsley has always been a place of arrival and settlement.

BUSES

I had a couple of driving lessons when I was seventeen years old because all my mates were getting them and I thought I should too. The driving instructor was more nervous than me and wore huge flapping sandals the size of narrowboats. Terrible tragicomic things happened during these driving lessons and then, minutes before the third one was due to begin, the instructor rang to cancel it 'on account of the fog'. Please believe me when I tell you that the day was clear and sunny and the visibility excellent. You could almost see the coast and Barnsley is almost as far away from the coast as you can get. I protested that it was clear as a bell in Darfield. 'It's pea soup here, kid, pea soup,' he said, his voice cracking with emotion. Or fear. Or Woodbines. I realised that he didn't want to carry on with my instruction and I put the phone down and concluded that driving was not for me and symbolically walked out of the house to the bus stop.

It was no great hardship to take the bus in those days because with Barnsley being part of the South Yorkshire Metropolitan Borough Council, otherwise known as the Socialist Republic of South Yorkshire, the buses were ridiculously cheap. The tale was that the councillor actually wanted to make the buses free but it was thought that they would then be undervalued by the passengers who had invested in the journey. The fact is that they may as well have been free: a trip to Barnsley from Darfield was 2p, and the cost of a slow rumble from Sheffield to Darfield was 10p. The buses were run by the wonderfully-named Yorkshire Traction Bus

Company, known locally as the Tracky Bus. My auntie's next door neighbour Mrs Beck was a conductress who could swing that set-rite ticket machine like a club and accidentally crack you on the back of the head if you gave her any lip, but she had a heart of gold. She was a fine example of the public-spirited conductors who would help you on with your shopping or your triplets, let you off with a penny or give you your change in bulging coin bags because you'd proffered a ten pound note for a 2p trip. Yorkshire Traction began rolling round the streets in 1902 as the Barnsley and District Electric Traction Company, running trams until 1930 by which time the word 'electric' had fallen from its name. The company dominated the public road transport of Barnsley and beyond, swallowing up several smaller outfits, presumably stunning them with Mrs Beck's Set-Rite first. I, for one, was sad to see the logo go from the side of the buses when they in turn were bought up by Stagecoach in 2005; there was something about that phrase Yorkshire Traction that just rang with Barnsley authenticity, something difficult to manufacture, but easy to spot if you keep your eyes and ears open.

The buses became my second home as I trundled around the villages of the Dearne Valley to see my various schoolmates and sometimes caught the endless epic bus the 70, which went from Sheffield to Upton, near Wakefield in West Yorkshire. My favourite bit of the journey was when the bus stopped in Wombwell to allow the driver off, to be replaced by another driver, like a 747 refuelling mid-Atlantic. Sometimes people wandered off the bus for a cigarette, got talking to a mate, and looked up to see it driving away with their shopping on the back seat.

The last bus home from Barnsley on a Friday or Saturday night was always a good natured riot with singing, dancing, snogging and once (it sounds like I'm making this up) a man playing the mouth organ who suddenly reached into his pocket and pulled out another instrument. 'Who knows that this is?' he shouted. Nobody knew. Frankly, nobody cared except me. 'It's an ocarina,' he shouted, 'I got it on my holidays', and he played it, causing it to create a strange and haunting sound all across the top deck. Once, during the miners' strike, on a packed bus that was making its way through slow market-day traffic to the town centre, a bloke stood up and read a long ballad-like poem about picketing.

Continuing the theme of Tracky Bus as UNESCO World Heritage site of Intangible Heritage, a man who came to one of my writing workshops in Barnsley once told me with huge seriousness that he had written the pilot script a TV series about a widowed cowboy and his three sons living on a ranch in the Wild West and had left it on the 222 bus from Doncaster to Barnsley and the next thing he knew 'There it was, Ian. My idea, on the telly: *Bonanza*! Never leave owt on a bus unless tha's copyrighted it!' I was going to tell him that the producers of *Bonanza* weren't often on the 222 but I've always been a fan of alternative histories so I let the fantasy fly.

The local equivalent of the 70 was the 13, which in later decades became the 213 and is now, at least in part, the 26. The 13 set off from Barnsley and eventually, after what seemed like long arid months, ended up in Doncaster. It went through Barnsley, Wombwell, Darfield, Middlecliffe, Little Houghton, Great Houghton, Thurnscoe, Goldthorpe and on (across the border so it need not concern us) into Doncaster. Doughty women in headscarves would sit for miles with pursed lips. Kids who were out for the day for 2p would flick tickets at each other. Travel-sick children would gaze out of the window trying to catch brief glimpses of any horizons that were on offer. A miner who'd missed the pit bus would sit there in his muck.

Ah, the pit bus; that was the other kind of bus that plied its steady way up and down the roads that ribboned the coalfield and the pit villages. Our school bus was one of Hargreaves's pit buses that had taken the day shift to Darfield Main before it picked us scholars up to take us to the grammar school. Much amusement was to be had when the older boys and girls were able to persuade the younger boys and girls to slap the seats with their rulers to make the coal dust fly, specking the white shirts and freckling the faces of the cream of Yorkshire's youth.

As I mentioned, I was a young teenager I was the drummer in the Folk-Rock band Oscar the Frog which rehearsed in Darfield Church Hall. After the practice the fiddle player, Steve Sutcliffe, would go to the roundabout in Darfield universally known as the Ring and catch the bus back home to Barnsley. Once, by mistake, he boarded the bus bringing a shift back from Houghton Main. The rest of us watched with a mixture of horror and glee as Steve stood at the front of the bus holding his violin, blinking back tears as the bus rocked with laughter and a wag shouted 'Hey, Paganini, does tha know any Cole Porter?'

A Deep Tarn Calendar – October

Kum eer. Ev a look.
Ev a look at this turnip
Av bin carvin
All afternooin.
What's tha reckon?
Ah meeean
Oooz tha reckon?
Oooz tha reckon, ey?
Tha reyt: it's Frank!
It's thi Uncle Frank!
Them teeeath
Them eees.
That grin.
He once purra candle in iz eead an all
Forra laff.
His mam woh blazin.
Ar. Like iz eead.

A Deep Tarn Calendar – November

Remember remember
When wi fust lit bonfire
An't smooak
Looked like a ghooast
Peeapin ovver
As them flames
Grew and grew
Lickin't sky
And chuckin sparks
Like confetti
Or reyt lickle torches.

A Deep Tarn Calendar – December

Then duz tha know what?
On't thirteenth day on Christmas
All them years sin
Ah gid her a tooilkit.
Well, she likes fettling and mending stuff.
She brok me art. The shi fettled it.
So ivvry Christmas when ivvrybodys
Gidoer messin wi prezents and all that
And young'uns ev snogged
Undert mizzletooer
Ah gee er a new summat
For't tooilkit.
This year it worra bandsaw.
Ah sez: ah know tha sharp enuff!
She laffed.
Ah luv it when she laffs.

SOUTH

LANGUAGE

This part of the book is partly geographically-specific and partly not; much of it could take place anywhere in the borough, but for the purposes of linguistic adventure let's begin here, on the other side of Birdwell. Birdwell is on the edge of the borough, at the top of Sheffield Road. A huge obelisk dominates the main street, acting as a sundial on warm summer days. People passing the obelisk often assume that it's another memorial to another pit disaster but in fact it's a monument to vanity, having been erected in 1775 for the second Earl of Strafford for no other reason, as far as I can see, than that it marks a point three miles from Wentworth Castle, the

folly-studded house and gardens built by and for the Earl. To me that's like dropping a banana skin three miles from your house and then getting a sculptor to make a bronze banana to commemorate the event and the place. I imagine him in one of the windows of the big house that's now Northern College. Pointing with a gloved hand at the obelisk, as his rotund mate strains to see beyond his lunch, he pipes 'Do you see that obelisk-shaped object there? That's three miles from here!'. For the country gent that was always the way: the earth was a series of places that either belonged to him or belonged to his mates. The Earl of Strafford liked his follies, as we've seen when we strolled around Wentworth Castle, and of course they're just versions of those old novelty wooden wheelbarrows full of flowers that you sometimes see in suburban gardens. Just bigger. And you can't make a sundial out of a novelty wooden wheelbarrow, unless it's a very bright day and you lean extremely close to the ground. I like the lost follies of this area (and indeed of any area) like the Lady's Folly that was situated on Tankersley Golf Course and demolished in 1960, the almost mythical Worsbrough Common Castle, and the pyramid-like structure in Blacker Hill called the Smoothing Iron.

Birdwell is also the home of another of Barnsley's many theatres, the fringe to the town's Civic and Lamproom, the Academy Theatre[1] which opened in 2004, fulfilling the dream of a stalwart of the local amateur operatic scene, Geoff Whitfield who had always wanted to run his own theatre. The Academy is on the site of an old freezer storage building and can often be heard reverberating to the sound of tap dancing, tribute band singing and plays. It's certainly a more useful memorial (although Geoff is still very much with us) than an obelisk that just tells you how far it is to your big, big house.

Beyond Birdwell are two small villages, Tankersley and Pilley, tucked away behind sheltering trees and always within earshot of the murmur and argument of the M1.

Pilley has entered comedy history not only because it has a resonant, giggle-inducing name which would sound different if you were Welsh, but because it was the birthplace in 1917 of the comedian Harry Worth,[2] whose 'both-sides-of-a-shop-window' routine used to make my Uncle Charlie laugh so much that he'd have to spit in the fire. The name of the village comes from old English words that, when rubbed together, make the name of a clearing in a wood where timber could be obtained; maybe Harry Worth's window comedy wasn't merely music hall but a long-buried folk-memory of the Pilley Timber Dance. Maybe.

Tankersley, just over the A61, feels ancient. Like much of this end of Barnsley it carries the footprint of those powerful families like the Straffords and the Fitzwilliams. The ruins of Tankersley Old Hall, which featured in the film *Kes*, otherwise known as the Barnsley Creation Myth, can be seen from the M1. They're in a sorry state these days but once they were a house that was the centre of a splendid deer park. Indeed Daniel Defoe, on his tour of England, wrote '...I saw the largest red deer that, I believe, are in this part of Europe: one of the hinds, I think, was larger than my horse...'. Those 'I believe's and 'I think's underline as far as I'm concerned

that Defoe was, like me, someone who never let the facts get in the way of a good story. The Hall may or may not have been destroyed during the Civil War in 1643, and there are cannonballs from the battle in the beautiful St Peter's Church which has, in the past, hosted an odd tradition called the 'Tankersley Clippings' that I often suspect was made up in the same way that the Up Helly Aa tradition in Shetland was. A local website says that the tradition 'is an ancient one that began in the 1920s and was revived in the 1970s' which doesn't, although I'm no historian, feel all that ancient to me. During the Clippings, which have also been called the Yclippings, the people of the village, including the schoolchildren, circle St Peter's Church on St Peter's Day, singing.

The thing that really interests me about Pilley, and Tankersley and Birdwell is that if you listened to those children you would detect that they came from Border Country, from disputed territory, from a line the other side of which, well, Here Be Dragons.

I could walk down the A61, on the pavement of course, from Tankersley, taking a diversion through Birdwell to look at the obelisk and try and catch a glimpse of Wentworth Castle, then through Hoyland Common, then through Platts Common and Jump (the place not the action) towards Hemingfield and Wombwell and the language would change subtly. I would pass through an isogloss, a small space where language changes. I would, in layman's terms, be strolling from the land of the Deedars to the land of the Dingles.

Barnsley people call Sheffield folk Deedars because they put a hard 'd' into words like 'thee' and 'tha'; for them, 'now then' becomes 'narden' and keen listeners like me can tell which side of the River Sheaf a speaker comes from. In Tankersley there's quite a lot of Narden and, excitingly for us accent-detectives, it fades away gradually as you go through Hoyland Common and make your way towards Platts Corner. Sheffielders call us 'Dingles' because they see themselves as big city sophisticates and they see us as slack-jawed country yokels like the Dingle Family on Emmerdale, the never-ending and disaster-prone White Rose soap. Both these ideas are both true and not true at the same time, which is the norm in the post-truth world of course.

Other locutions are, it seems to me, peculiar to Barnsley. The use of Yore, for example, meaning 'you lot' or just 'you'. 'How are you?' you'll say to man in a cap who is leaning on a wall. 'Or 8' he'll say, 'How yore?' and it won't matter if you're on your own or you're with your wife, you're still Yore. In some parts of Yorkshire they say 'reet' when they mean 'right' but in Barnsley we say 'Reyt', which is a hyper-local shard of language, it seems to me. There may, of course, be another isogloss, a reyt/reet one, towards the north of the borough where South Yorkshire brushes very gently up against West Yorkshire.

In Barnsley we say 'Heyop' not 'Heyup' and we say 'frame thissen' if we want people to shape up. Despite our flat and flinty vowels we say Naow, a little bit like a laryngitis meow, when we say no, and we never, ever say lunch, unless we say it with flapping exaggerated air quotes. We have Dinner and Dinner at Teatime. As you go through this book, imagine the people around you using these words. Imaging them saying 'I were stood theer like Clem' and 'I were stood theer like Souse' and 'I'll stand for 't'egg under t'cap.' It's a language that comes from deep earth and the Vikings and industry and post-industry. Barnsley people are reputed to be dour, and perhaps we are, but I think you should listen carefully, as though you're straining for a mole coming to the surface or pressing a glass to a wall in a hotel room for sounds of a whispered argument. We're all poets really; it's just that the music is minimal. Let's move on, before we start sounding like deedars. Dat would never do, would it?

ELSECAR

It's funny how much Elsecar has grown and mutated in my mind and in the popular imagination. For decades my relationship with it was a rail-based one. I saw it as a stop on the train from Barnsley to Sheffield that I once got off at by mistake when I'd nodded off and thought I was arriving in Wombwell. When me and my mate, the late Martyn Wiley, presented a Saturday morning show on BBC Radio Sheffield in the 1980s we once saw a bloke sitting on a white faux-leather settee on Platform 1 and we riffed about it for a good ten minutes and got people to ring in about furniture on stations. For many years there was an old derelict Beverley Bar bus[3] in an allotment visible from the train, and during the miners' strike of 1984-85 you saw people coal picking on a low hill near the station. It was also, (and still is to a lesser extent) amusing to hear posh/automated train announcements referring to 'Elsie Carr' who sounds like a chapel-goer who worked part time in a sweetshop.

These days, though, Elsecar is talked about (mainly by me and other history-enthusiasts, I must admit) as a future UNESCO World Heritage Centre, with visitors flocking from all over the world and getting off the train and ignoring the settee. The reason for this is the presence that pervades this book and settles over the

borough like one of those teatowels my mam used to put over the canary's cage every night: Earl Fitzwilliam of Wentworth Woodhouse. Without him and his pals and their vision and the sweat of men and women in caps and bonnets this part of the world would have looked and felt very different.

I get off the train and walk down to the Elsecar Heritage Centre[4] that a lot of the older people round here still call the NCB workshops; the site is full of listed buildings and was taken over by Barnsley Council in 1988 and opened as a Heritage Centre at a time when the idea of tourists coming to this part of the world seemed like something from the first draft of a Monty Python sketch. I sometimes take a detour, if I want to remember my dancing days, past the site of the old nite-spot (sic) The Birdcage, a haunt of under-age drinking and the source of many epic anecdotes that pushed Saturday night into Sunday morning with baroque riffs and 'he said/she said' trills.

Elsecar Heritage Centre contains so many important historic sites it's difficult to know where to begin, but I always start at the Newcomen Beam Engine, the only working example of its kind still *in situ* in the world. The engine was built to pump water out of the deep and damp Elsecar New Colliery which was sunk by the fourth Earl Fitzwilliam in 1795. Like much industrial archaeology, it's a remarkable survivor, weathering weather and neglect and the possibility of theft and vandalism. It drew up to 600 gallons of water a minute from the pit, to enable deeper and deeper seams to be dug and remarkably (I use that word a lot when I'm talking about Elsecar) was driven by steam until 1923. I like to imagine the constant pounding of the Newcomen giving a half-noticed rhythm to Elsecar's days and nights: citizens trying not to walk in step with it but failing miserably; people talking to the beat like an early version of hip-hop.

The main building in the suite of constructions around the Elsecar Heritage site is the workshops, originally built to co-ordinate all the mending and fixing and small-scale banging and hammering that needed doing on the estate and after nationalisation became the hub of metal-bashing for all the pits in the area. They closed in the early 1980s.

I wander down to the Elsecar Steam Railway, a preserved line originally built by Earl Fitzwilliam to transport iron and coal to the main line. I can catch the train on Sundays and also catch a glimpse of what it might have been like in the days when this part of the world was a true Northern Powerhouse of the Industrial

Revolution. If it's December you can also get a present from Father Christmas, perhaps mirroring what the Earl himself would have done. Perhaps.

What excites me and others about the possibility of this whole site is that the iron, the coal, the railway, the road and the canal are in such close proximity, preserving a snapshot of the lost and forgotten times in a way that feels like Ironbridge in Shropshire or Saltaire in West Yorkshire. Walk by the canal on a sunny day and try and place yourself in the middle of the industrial revolution; it's not easy because the only sounds are those of an ice cream van and a barking dog, but it's possible if you shut your eyes. Don't go too near the water, obviously.

The canal at Elsecar was a branch from the Dearne and Dove Canal[5] which made its steady way from Swinton to Barnsley and had two branch-lines, or branch streams; one at Worsbrough and one at Elsecar. The Elsecar one is in much better condition than the Worsbrough branch, which is almost entirely overgrown. Over the years enthusiasts and volunteers have talked about re-opening this particular section of the Super Slow Way but for the moment we'll have to just enjoy it as a knife blade reflecting the sky and cutting through the earth.[6] The canal basin at Elsecar has a kind of majesty, and you can more easily imagine the barges taking and bringing things from the huge works here. These days fishermen sit for hours like still street theatre performers at the Edinburgh Fringe, and people who've got a bike for Christmas whizz by, their new helmets polished and gleaming.

As I write this, new slabs of history are being discovered; huge blast furnaces from the ironworks can be seen in nineteenth century photographs and part of the ironworks buildings form the engine shed of the Heritage Railway; at the back of the main Heritage Centre there are a row of disused buildings that are part of the ironworks. Each time I visit Elsecar another layer of history has been peeled away. Watch this UNESCO space!

HOYLAND

Between Wombwell and Junction 36 of the M1, you'll come to Hoyland and Hoyland Common and Hoyland Nether but not High Hoyland because that's somewhere else in a different part of the borough. In one place you've got all the Hoylands except one. The word Hoyland is an ancient one and it means 'a farm on a hill' but it's unusual that a great concentration of the Hoylands in the country are in this part of the world, farms dotting the hills like sheep before the coal was found and shovelled out of the floor. When I was a young man Hoyland Nether had its own Urban District Council, like a number of the towns and villages in the borough and was only called Hoyland Nether to distinguish it from High Hoyland, which isn't as high as Hoylandswaine, but that's another story in another part of the book. In the end, Hoyland and Hoyland Common and Hoyland Nether are all really segments of the same place but don't tell the people who live there that.

The most striking architectural feature of this part of Barnsley is Hoyland Lowe Stand, which isn't Lowe, it's high, because it's said to be the highest point in South Yorkshire. I promise I'll stop soon. This building which is listed but is in an advanced state of decay, was originally a hunting lodge and observatory for the ubiquitous Marquess of Rockingham, one of the Wentworths who spread like upper-class bindweed across the county. The neglect of the building is tragic and despite the valiant efforts of yet another friends group, the Friends of Lowe Stand, could only be seen to be getting worse with the internal spiral staircase almost gone, but as you walk or drive by it you can imagine how magnificent it would once have been. I'm not sure that it really is the highest point in the county because there must be places nearer the clouds around Penistone or on the wilder fringes of Sheffield but when you stand by the Stand and the wind flaps the notebook in your hand then you feel high, really high. You could almost be a Wentworth and you wonder whether any trace of any Wentworth DNA is floating around your greying quiff and giving you a kind of toff-glow.

Hoyland is known as the birthplace of the great South Yorkshire (and beyond) novelist and anti-toff Barry Hines who was born there in 1939. The novel *A Kestrel For A Knave* pervades Barnsley like *Moby Dick* pervades Nantucket. I remember once going on a stroll with him down the streets he used to play in as a child to record his musings and recreate a feeling for the place for a radio programme. He was enthusing about the walls he kicked the ball into and the alleys he hid from the grownups down when we noticed an older man in a flat cap digging a garden as though he was a dictionary definition of the word stolid. He regarded us in the same way a boiled egg might look at a spoon. Actually, although Barry isn't with us any more, I can imagine him telling me off for using the word 'regarded' when I could have said 'looked at'. 'We don't regard, Ian lad,' he would say, his voice revving up as he got into his stride, 'we look at things. We just look at them.' The older man looked at him and pushed the cap back on his gleamingly-domed head. 'Hello,' said Barry eagerly, sticking his hand over the fence for the man to shake. The man looked at the hand as though it was a fish that had come out of the fryer in the chip shop too soon. 'We know who thy are,' he said, the air withering around him.

Hoyland Common and Platts Common weren't really villages until after the enclosure act; they remained as farming settlements until the pits were sunk and houses were built for miners and nailers who would make nails and then take them down to Lincolnshire by cart. Like many of the villages in the area, once the miners came, Hoyland became a boom-town Klondyke, indeed, a contemporary writer noted that 'The village of Hoyland Common seems to be improving with something of the speed observable in American towns' as the local mines flourished. Miners from here would work at Elsecar, at Barrow Colliery, a huge pit with three shafts, Hoyland Silkstone Colliery which was situated at Platts Common, Lidgett Colliery, Rockingham Colliery and Hemingfield Pit.

Not much remains of any of these enterprises, although the engine houses for the Lidgett Colliery, a small pit which shut well before nationalisation, are used as a garage and can be seen by the side of the road that leads up to Hoyland Common from Harley. Hemingfield Pit, a tiny mine near Elsecar, is being lovingly restored by, yes, a group of volunteers called Friends of Hemingfield Pit who hold fortnightly open days and who are determined to make this site part of the archaeological ecology of the town.

JUMP

Jump isn't twinned with anywhere because there's nowhere else in the world called Jump. There might be somewhere on a distant planet at the far edge of the galaxy called Jump but I really doubt it. Of course, when you visit Barnsley, of even if you've lived there for a long, long time, you should always catch the bus to Jump just so that you can say 'Is this bus gunner Jump?' and then when the driver says, 'Yes' with a weary heard-it-all-before nod of the head, you can say 'Well hold it down while I get on'. Maybe, in a perfect, world, the driver's brother, a bus driver in Merseyside, will be saying the same tired 'Yes' to someone who's just said 'Is this bus gunner Speke?' just so the passenger can say 'Well tell it to shurrup while I get on.'

The real reason that Jump is so called is a little obscure but the consensus seems to be that it comes from the local miners having to jump across the stream to get to the one of the pits at Elsecar, although there's a holier version that states that the congregation had to jump over the same stream to get to the church. Let's all imagine a contemporary dance piece showing the miners going one way and the churchgoers going the other way.

Like much of this part of the world, Jump is an ancient settlement, and when the new estate was being built at Roebuck Hill in the village by Persimmon Homes, archaeologists found remains of an early Iron Age roundhouse, a late Iron Age or early Roman farmstead and further evidence of the creeping tide of industrialisation as farming was superseded on the hill by small-scale industrialisation. What's the Latin for 'Is this chariot gunner Jump?'

Jump bumps into Hemingfield, the next village along, and also a village that would have supplied the local mines with workers. The school there is listed in a nineteenth century directory as a Charity School, and its crest bears the legend The Educational Foundation of George Ellis 1711.

George Ellis was a local benefactor from Brampton near Rotherham; he provided money for lectures in the nearby town of Wath, for the church at Darfield, and for two schools in Brampton, as well as for the Ellis School in Hemingfield. Brampton isn't that close to Hemingfield within the micro-topography of the area, so I'm at a loss as to why he funded a school there and not in, say Wath.

Elsecar Heritage Railway terminates at Hemingfield but on the way you get a sense of the importance of the route in the days when coal and iron were being produced in the powerhouse that was Elsecar; as you approach Hemingfield you'll spot the colliery

buildings that are described elsewhere in these pages and the twin barge mooring basins that were used to load the coal. Hemingfield Pit is a real survivor, in the process of being restored by a group of volunteers.[7]

To wander (carefully) around the partially-restored Hemingfield Pit is to get a sense of how important it would have been for the Elsecar industries; its own loading basin was superseded by the Elsecar Railway where it was possible for coal straight from the mine to be loaded straight onto the passing train wagons.

MUSIC

Music transcends considerations of Barnsley geography, and because I've always been interested in music and perhaps because I've (ahem) performed a little myself, as the Tupperware basher in Oscar the Frog in the 1970s, I'm interested in the places that people get together to hear music so let's bring the *Real Barnsley* floodlight to bear on the musical hotspots in the town, bearing in mind that the scene is constantly changing so that by the time you read this you may as well be gazing at the Rosetta Stone. I like unofficial venues, pop-up spaces that are here today but unless you're quick they're gone tomorrow before you've had time to tune your guitar.

Wombwell is, at the moment, a hotbed of musical endeavour. Each Summer the Womfest takes over most of the local pubs with bands in the Alma, the Prince of Wales, the Old Town Hall, Squires Bar and lots of points in between. When I passed through last July the event was, to use an old-fashioned phrase, in full swing, and was spilling out onto the streets and car parks. A band was pumping out heavy rhythms in the Alma car park, and some people were either dancing or demonstrating how to put up a deckchair on Cleethorpes beach in the face of a force ten gale. There's long been a tradition of live music in the Prince of Wales, a pub at the top of Station Lane that looks down towards Low Valley; I remember when I was at the tennis-ball factory in town in the early 1980s somebody from Wombwell whiling away a quiet night shift remembering the time in the 60s when a jazz-rock band played and the drummer outstayed his welcome with his solo which went on longer than the career of many Barnsley managers until either a disgusted drinker or a fellow band member took umbrage and hurled him out of the window onto the main street.

Barnsley's music scene was for many years dominated by the working men's clubs which put on bands and solo artists a number of nights and lunchtimes in the week and at weekends and supported a thriving music scene; the clubs have declined but on a recent weekend, taken at random, you can see Face the Music at the Royston Klondyke, Beardsmith at the Trades Club and The Moode at Monk Bretton WMC. Here are real musicians working hard to entertain; it's easy for people to sneer at these kinds of clubs but if they worked to a fraction of their potential we wouldn't need arts centres or libraries, but don't tell the government that.

The folk scene is alive and well with the Barnsley Folk Club putting on gigs at the newly refurbished Old School House venue, which used to be the Polish Club up Summer Lane on the way to the hospital. My youth was misspent in Barnsley's many folk clubs; on Saturday nights I would go to the club at the Centenary Rooms at the Civic Hall with the girl who has been my wife for many decades. I remember the Saturdays there with a glow that must be more than nostalgia's sepia flame. I remember, too, the reason we stopped going, which was odd in the extreme: the MC announced that the next Saturday was to be 'Balls, Banquets and Functions' and I, stupidly, took this to mean that a private party, perhaps a wedding, was taking over the rooms. This wasn't the case and it was actually a band called Balls Banquets and Functions who were appearing. Tradition, as somebody once said, is a flame that once snuffed out cannot be rekindled, and from then we simply stopped going.

THE SCRAPYARD LION AND THE WHALE

Every town should have its mythical and not so mythical creatures; Holmfirth isn't too far from Barnsley and there they've got the tale of Fenella the Tiger, a circus performer who ended up living in the garden of a terraced street in that quiet West Yorkshire town. Older denizens of Doncaster still tell the tale of the time the bear escaped from the grotto-cum-zoo in the middle of town and people ran to take shelter in the entrance hall of the girls' grammar school.

The two real/legendary animals in Barnsley are the Klondyke Lion and the Barnsley Whale. Both flicker at the edge of Barnsley's eyeballs as it sleeps at night; both are half-remembered and half-forgotten at the same time. Both culminate in tales of eccentricity and/or endeavour, depending on your point of view.

The Barnsley Whale really was forgotten until Barnsley fan Steve Deput began researching it towards the end of the last millennium. Steve had vague memories of seeing the whale on the back of a lorry sometime in the 1960s and he set about asking fellow BFC fans on the internet if they remembered it. Many didn't and some thought the whole thing was a windup, but eventually other whale-rememberers began to gather in cyberspace and the Barnsley Whale hove into view like Moby Dick appearing at the side of Gregory Peck's beady eye in the film of the same name. That's the film *Moby Dick*, not the film Beady Eye.

Steve, in his own words, became obsessed: 'I left my job in London and toured the country asking my questions in pubs, on the street and in museums. Rather than ignore me or laugh down the phone, people could do it in my face.' Eventually Steve contacted Vanessa Toulmin from the National Fairground Archive at the University of Sheffield and she pointed him to the proof.

It turned out that the whale had been caught of Trondheim in Norway in 1952 and had toured the world for decades, ostensibly to begin with as an advert for whaling, as Norway and the rest of Europe started to rebuild their shattered economies after World War Two, but the sight of the dead whale, as Steve pointed out, probably put more people off. For a quarter of a century the whale (it was called Jonah but I prefer to call it Malcolm) traversed the globe on the back of a specially-built truck that at 100 feet long was one of the biggest in the world at that time. In a poignant touch, a dead dormouse perched on Malcolm's nose in a tiny glass case (I'm 61 and I've never written that sentence before) to act, like working class people often did on the first photographs, as a unit of scale. And Malcolm (Jonah) was one a trio of itinerant whales, along with Goliath and Hercules, or as I prefer to call them Trevor and Derek.

So, in the end, Barnsley was just one of a number of towns that Malcolm visited, which both shrinks and expands the legend, in my opinion. Each place has its own particular take on the localness and mysteriousness of the leviathan, and without the diligence of people like Steve, the story would have remained untold, would just have flashed across peoples' heads as they strolled through Locke Park or waited for a late bus.

Robert Warburton on a BBC website remembers the whale being parked 'where Littlewoods and BHS were in Barnsley centre. It stank. It looked like it was covered in tar and the front saw the gaping mouth with what looked like tassels for teeth. Someone said that it was to be destroyed at Soot Hill, Dewsbury and someone said that when it was burnt the kiln exploded due to the gases, but this whale must have stirred more rumours. Happy days!'

Steve assumed the whale had been destroyed but it turned up in Belgium where a circus boss called Mike Austen kept it under tarpaulin. Steve visited the warehouse where it was kept and wrote 'there in the yard was the same tarpaulin-covered lorry I'd seen forty years ago. Rolling back the covers there lay Jonah as huge and awe-inspiring as I remembered.' I think that phrase 'as huge and awe-inspiring as I remembered' is a good metaphor for books like these; not that they're necessarily huge and/or awe inspiring, but the memories they generate certainly can be.

The other semi-mythical member of the Barnsley menagerie, the Klondike Lyon, used to guard a scrapyard in that part of Barnsley between Monk Bretton and Cudworth known as the Klondyke, presumably because in the heady days of the early coal-rush it must have resembled a Wild West town without the wide-brimmed hats and tumbleweed. There is a western connection to this tale, mind you.

A scrap dealer called Dennis Higgs kept the lion to ward off intruders; the tale was that he'd got this guard-Leo from a travelling circus and it was very useful in keeping intruders away. In 2010 Dennis bought a ranch in Cheyenne, Wyoming, because, as it said in the *Yorkshire Post* at the time, 'he fancied a new challenge after spending his life building up his business in Barnsley'. Oil was found on the ranch, the proceeds from which would, it was said at the time, make Dennis into a multimillionaire. In typical understated Barnsley fashion, he was quoted as saying 'I'm not planning on doing anything wild or crazy and neither is the family. It's just one of those things that happens but I can't deny it's good news.' In fact I have to say that I think that is one of the most Barnsley statements ever, and could be used as a template for all things Barnsley, rivalling the wonderful ur-Barnsley moment I once witnessed at Oakwell when the ball spun into the crowd from a miskick, an elderly man stood up, took off his flat cap, headed the ball back to the astonished player, and then put his flat cap back on.

The Whale and the Lion: it's a Barnsley pub name waiting to happen.

WORTLEY AND HOWBROOK

Years ago I would map the contours of my life through bellringing, a hobby that became an obsession for me and so whenever I went through a village I would see if it had a church, and if I had time I would stop and see if the village had a ringable peal of bells. I know. I must have been insufferable. Sometimes I would leave a note for the vicar, explaining that we could rid his tower of pigeon detritus and make his bells ringable again.

Wortley, on the border of Barnsley and Sheffield, had a fine ring of eight bells and me and the other Darfield Bellringers would often go over to their practice night or to ring for a wedding.[8] One day me and a couple of the lads, (that'll be Noel Marsden and Dave Sunderland and maybe Steve Cameron) decided to walk from Darfield to Wortley, a distance of almost ten miles, just to prove that we could. We thought it would be a bit of an adventure and a bit of a daft thing to do, to turn up to ring on a Sunday evening having just walked to the venue. It was a red hot day in 1976, that sweltering summer, and so in my memory Wortley is always warm, and it's full of sweating people and people mopping their brows and glugging from vast bottles of pop the size of fire extinguishers. In my memory Wortley is about aching feet and a sense of despair as me and the lads sat on a bench and realised we'd only got as far as Wombwell, which, if Wortley was the summit of Everest, was the basecamp.

The other thing I remember about our Wortley walk was that we'd not worked out how we were getting back and the cars that brought the other, more sensible bellringers were all full and my long-suffering dad had to be persuaded to leave his gardening to bring us home.

Wortley isn't always hot, of course; not everybody sweats there. It's a tiny village just off the A61 that's the home of Wortley Hall, a magnificent big house the strapline of which is 'The Workers' Stately Home'.[9] It's yet another of the enormous dwellings that dot the whole of the Barnsley borough in various states of repair and importance; this one's history is very interesting and its present and future are perhaps even more so. It has been built and rebuilt over many centuries and the latest rebuilding happened at the start of the nineteenth century when James Archibald Edward Wortley and his wife Caroline moved into the house. They extended and renovated the house during the Victorian period but during the Second World

War the army occupied part of the house and after 1945 it began to crumble and fray at the edges. In 1950 the Wharncliffe family decided to give up the house and, galvanised by the contemporary political ferment and the 'we-are-the-masters-now' feeling that was abroad at the time, a group of labour movement activists led by a local man called Vin Williams bought the house and in 1951 it was opened as a holiday and educational centre for the trade union and wider labour movement.

The last time my wife and I visited Wortley Hall was to a plant fair, much to the amusement of our children who thought it was both a quaint and a ludicrous exercise. Wandering around inside, you gasp at the amazing high ceilings in the dining room and the astonishing gardens that are currently being restored and looked after by volunteers.

The village itself is tiny and dominated by the church (if you look carefully you can still see drops of my sweat darkening the steps from the walk we did in 1976. No you can't.) and the pub, the Wortley Arms. The church is beautiful and serene and dotted with memorials to the landowners of the area and the pub, which was originally an eighteenth-century coach house, was once the place where my fellow bellringers and I supped ale and talked about Grandsire Doubles, and the best way to ring down after a quarter peal, and its now a place of fine, fine dining. There's also the Wortley Men's Club and Institute, which was revived recently and is now winning awards for its beer and hospitality, and the Countess Tea Rooms. I look in vain for a plaque celebrating me and fellow

campanologists' walk there in what was officially The Last Hot Summer We Ever Had but it'll come, it'll come.

The defining legend of Wortley is that of the Dragon of Wantley, a St George-style legend of a dragon-slaying on Wharncliffe Crags just outside the village which were recounted in a seventeenth-century broadsheet ballad and a nineteenth-century novel by Owen Wister, the author of that western classic *The Virginian*. I made a radio programme about it a few years ago which convinced me that perhaps the legend was true. Mind you, I also thought *The Virginian* was true.

Wortley Top Forge (despite its name, it's not all that close to Wortley) is, amazingly, the oldest surviving heavy iron forge in the world; it was built in 1640s and was still working until a few years before the First World War. The industrial site was abandoned between the wars although the cottages built for the workers were still occupied until the 1960s.

Over many years a tale of neglect and decay has become a story of hope as the South Yorkshire Industrial History Society have painstakingly (although I'm sure they enjoy it) restored the original water wheels and water-powered drop hammers. I don't know what the collective noun for a group of steam mill engines is, but there's a suite of them at Wortley Top Forge, all either working or in the process of being restored. The Wortley Top Forge Model Engineers have also built a miniature railway that you ride on round the site which, for men like me, is something that gets you very close to the sublime. Make a Sunday of it: walk to Wortley from Darfield. Ring some bells. Walk on Wharncliffe Crags in search of the Dragon's Cave. Buy some plants at Wortley Hall as the laughter of your children echoes in your ears. Spread a napkin on your knee in the dining room of the Wortley Arms. Get some steam in your hair on the back of a miniature railway. Glug micro-brewed ale in the Wortley Men's Club, even if you're not a man. Chew a scone in the Countess Tea Rooms. I read on their Facebook page: 'A wasp landed on my scone and the waitress didn't hesitate and brought me another one.' Now that's the kind of service that makes you buzz.

BUYING RECORDS

I'm 61 years old so when I was a teenager my main activity, apart from thinking about Diana Rigg as Emma Peel and wishing that she lived in Darfield, was buying records. Woolworth's on Wombwell High Street was the place to buy singles and EPs; I remember my brother coming home once with 'Ghost Riders In The Sky' by Marty Robbins in a paper bag. We played it over and over again on the Dansette until my mother said 'I'll give you 'Ghost Riders In The Sky' in a minute' in the way that all mams would just tell you what you were doing and add the words 'I'll give you', and 'in a minute…' to give the misdemeanour added gravitas. 'I'll give you throwing crusts around in a minute!' for example, or 'I'll give you are we nearly there yet in a minute!' It usually had the desired effect, but not with 'Ghost Riders in the Sky', which we carried on playing till bedtime.

The shops in Wombwell were okay if you wanted 'Ramona' by The Bachelors but me and my mates preferred a more mature retail destination, although we didn't know that's what they were called then, and that's why we went to Barnsley to buy our LPs. Sometimes we went on the LP bus to buy our LPs and when we pointed this out to each other we thought we were so cool that we were almost glacial.

We frequented two record shops in particular: Neal's Music in The Arcade (now called The Victorian Arcade as we move further away from the Victorian era) and the uber-sharp Casa Disco next to the toilets in Peel Square. Neal's Music Shop sold musical instruments and sheet music as well as records. It was the sort of place your dad went for his Jim Reeves records whereas the Casa Disco, so called because it sold cassettes and discs, was the place to hang around if you were in a band, or wanted to be in a band, or dreamed of wanting to be in a band. There were handwritten notices on a board asking for 'bass players for soul-funk outfit based in Cundy Cross' or 'Machine Death Rust seek female vocalist; own transport essential'. Oddly, when I told people at North Staffordshire Polytechnic, my Higher Education institution of choice, that my local record shop was called the Casa Disco, they laughed at its naivety and unsophistication, its creakingly-faux worldy-wisdom. They came from sophisticated places like Kidderminster or Egremont, so I suppose they'd know.

The ultimate dad moment in Neal's Music happened when my dad went to buy me the LP *Lick My Decals Off, Baby* by the mighty Captain Beefheart for my fifteenth birthday. He told me that he'd be embarrassed to ask the lady in the shop, as he referred to her, so he wrote a note with the words on, presented it to the shocked Saturday girl behind the counter, and Mr Neal had to be sent for and the police were almost called. It wasn't as good as *Trout Mask Replica* either.

One of the things at the top of a small town wish-list is a record shop that can serve as an alternative youth club, Aladdin's Cave, beat generation freight car, and horizon-widening laboratory. They were places where you could grow up in public, could make your mistakes and buy records that you took back the week after and tried to pretend that they wouldn't play or you could make discoveries that would stay with you for the rest of your life. The Casa Disco had listening booths too; private spaces with Jodrell Bank-sized headphones that you could sit in and sink into your own private universe that was always better than the real one outside.

It was in one of these cramped booths that I discovered the album that became the soundtrack of the courting days of my wife when she was my girlfriend. I'd heard some of *Valentyne Suite* by Colosseum on the John Peel show on Radio 1 but sadly my batteries had gone before the immense (in all kinds of ways) track reached its end. I took it from the rack (I secretly loved that transgressive Y in Valentyne), sat in the booth and listened to the whole thing, nodding my head and possibly (forgive me) snapping my fingers.

I finally stepped out of the booth and put the record back in its place because I was short of the money to buy it until my next shift at Ernest Wiley's factory. The owner of the Casa Disco fixed me with a stare that could have filleted haddock and said 'Never, and I mean never, do that again!' and I walked out of the shop skulking and sunset-red.

FIELD MAPS

Of course, every other week and sometimes on Tuesday evenings I make my way to Oakwell to watch the mighty Barnsley F.C. but for years every Sunday morning I also made my way, my wife driving and me clutching a printed map or a fading satnav on a phone that I'd forgotten to charge up, across the borough to watch my grandson play football. He's given up the football now, and he plays cricket, so the hunt for various junior Theatres of Dreams is still on but this time you know that if it's raining or cold (I know cricket is a summer game but it's often raining or cold) you can get into a clubhouse and sit with a cup of tea.

A book like this is a kind of unofficial map of a place, but then there are even more unofficial maps that have a relationship to the book like the Edinburgh Fringe has to the Edinburgh International Festival or Broadway to Off- and Off-Off-Broadway.

His home ground when he played football for the Brierley Cubs was at Brierley Park. If we arrived early enough, which we often did, we'd witness Les the Ice Cream Man putting the nets up; my daughter would be setting up the rickety table that held what, even in South Yorkshire, they called The Tuck Shop; the teams would be warming up and the parents would be standing around or sitting on garden chairs they'd brought from home. Sometimes a scout from a League One or a Championship or, sometimes, a Premiership team would turn up and the lads and girls would hog the ball and never pass and attempt astonishing pirouettes or daring free kicks that often ended up in mud-sculptures or the ball sailing into the gardens of the nearby streets.

Darfield Cricket Club, his home club, is at the centre of the village opposite the Conservative Club and Amy's Chinese Takeaway; it's a handsome ground with a row of trees partly shielding it from the road and a line of fairly uncomfortable benches to sit on. The street behind the club is called Cover Drive, revealing a council planner with a sense of humour, although the street behind Cover Drive is called Norville Crescent, which reveals a council planner with a very limited sense of humour. Because I'm a certain kind of Yorkshireman there's nothing I like better than perching on one of these benches and watching a match as the late afternoon sun fires up the windows of the houses across the valley towards Great Houghton. It seems to me that a football ground (although I love football) can be a place of shouting and shoving, but a cricket ground can be a place of scattered applause and a sudden take-off of pigeons as a ball flies by. Having said that, I once saw Darfield play against a team whose strike bowler, a man in his late 40s, shouted the word 'Shit!' at the end of his explosive run-up just before he released the ball. At first I thought he was sneezing but then I realised he was using strong language. I listened, fascinated, to see if he did it each time and, over after over, he did. They could hear him on Cover Drive and beyond.

Barnsley, like any other small town, is dotted with cricket and football clubs which speak volumes (if we'd only listen) about the way that people need to get together to play sports or watch people play sports or talk about people playing sports. Sometimes we'd go and watch our grandson playing football or cricket at the Shaw Lane Sporting Complex, founded in 1862 near the old Boy's Grammar School. Over the years the complex has grown from when it used to just house rugby and cricket to the point where you can now play football on the top field, there's a hockey team and squash courts and archery targets. The football fields are at the top of a slope and the winds there appear to have been imported specially from the Arctic. At one freezing game the players and the referee and the assistant referees ran and shivered at the same time as though they'd invented a new dance; the wind was so strong that it blew the tuck table over and everyone was so cold that for a while, nobody bothered to try to pick it up, even though picking it up would have improved our circulation.

In the 1960s the club hosted a number of Yorkshire's one day Benson and Hedges matches, and sometimes the Yorkshire second team play there and I for one look forward to the day when Yorkshire play there again and a ball falls towards me from high in the air and I leap like a grey-haired salmon/gazelle cross and catch it. 'Sign him up!' somebody shouts.

Local football teams like Shaw Lane Aquaforce, Athersley Rec and Penistone Church are expanding their facilities and attracting bigger crowds as people are priced out of Championship matches. At Athersley Rec for example, you only pay a few pounds to get in to the cosy Sheerien Park ground and you're treated to a high level of football and an even higher level of passion. The ground can fit 2000 fans in, 420 covered and 150 seated; I'm a fan of so-called non-league football grounds (because every team everywhere is in a league) and Sheerien Park is a fine example, as is Penistone

Church F.C., founded in 1906 and playing in a lovely position on the edge of the town at the Memorial Ground.

If you were to draw a map of the borough using only football and cricket grounds you'd get a fascinating view of the place; each Sunday morning you'd be able to trace activity via the numbers of cars rushing from village to village trying to find the ground of the day. Other maps you could try could include the routes of ice cream vans, lost dogs.

THE DOCTORS

I'm lucky in that, unlike many people who live round here, I've managed to keep my health. 'Fighting fit!' my dad used to say, rubbing his belly and patting his head at the same time, as though it was some kind of folk cure for all ailments from his native Lanarkshire.

When I was younger, there were often people around the borough who would be described by my auntie as Poorly Folks. There were fewer vast, or morbidly obese, human beings around than there are now and if we saw anybody who was huge we were urged not to stare. 'It'll be glandular,' my mother would say under her breath, although my Uncle Charlie used to say, loudly, 'Glandular? It's Aleular!', a word he made up and that I never understood until much later in life. You would often see old miners just pausing in their morning walk, stopping to catch their breath because their lungs had been wrestled to the ground by years of working at the coalface. They wheezed like squeaky shed doors and if they saw you looking at them they'd point to their hearts and say 'Chesser's gone, kid. Beamshaw seam.' They'd say those last two words like 'Beeeamsher Seeeam' and then they'd spit on the floor and set off again, slowly, slowly.

There were also men, in those utopian days of near-full male employment, who, again in the words of my auntie, 'wouldn't have it'. In other words, they didn't work, which was the equivalent of a bear not shitting in the woods. They would limp round the village using sticks that some people insisted were props. They would be seen at bus stops at times of the day when men were never seen at bus stops unless it was a Sunday or there was a strike on. Occasionally, if an ambulance passed, they would sneeze. Probably these men had genuine illnesses but they were often looked on by the community like Tory governments look on disabled people.

When I was a boy I had terrible hay fever; just a drawing of a lawn being cut would send me into fireworks of sneezing. My mam and dad took me to our doctor in Thurnscoe, where the bluff but kindly Doctor Allison sat me down and drew circles on my forearm with a biro and sat back. I smiled at him and said I felt better already and got up to go. He laughed. He then explained (although I could hardly hear him for my rising tide of sobbing) that he was going to make a small hole in my arm at each of the places where he'd drawn the circle with a number of pins; in each of the pins there would be a sample of what I might be allergic to. The small hole that became reddest would indicate my allergy. 'I'm allergic to grass,' I said, hoping to deflect the oncoming pain. 'Yes,' he said, with a twinkle in his eye that spoke about years at medical school, 'but what kind of grass?' After a while one throbbing red area on my pasty arm showed him which kind of grass. I thought that was the end of my ordeal, but I was wrong again. Doctor Allison put me on a course of injections which meant that for the next nine months my dad had to take me to Thurnscoe once a week and watch me blubber as the doctor punctuated my arm until I looked like the surface of one of the minor moons of Jupiter. My dad often took pity on me and bought me a plastic animal from the shop near the surgery to staunch the flow of tears so that by the end of the course not only was I not sneezing but I had enough animals to start a zoo.

Years later I broke my leg on the way home from school, pausing on my walk up the Inkerman Fields with my auntie to kick a huge snowball that turned out to have a rock underneath it. My auntie, a frail woman with inner steel, carried the lump of me home and my dad drove me to Doctor Allison's, making sure he had enough change to buy me a baboon. 'You've done a greenstick!' the doctor boomed, as though I was a folk dancer.

When I was older we registered with the doctors in Darfield; it always seemed odd that our doctor was in Thurnscoe, a few miles away, but that was historically to do with my mother coming from Great Houghton. If you lived here you'd understand. Think of it as a board game involving the 14 bus and the 37 bus.

I turned out for my Wath Grammar School Under 15s rugby team against a team from a school in Rotherham which purported to consist of fellow teenagers but whose members seemed to have come straight up from Thrybergh pit. In the scrum, one of these boy-men attempted to remove my eye from its socket and rubbed his rough stubble on my soft bardic cheeks. The stubble hurt more than the gouging, oddly, and has remained more vivid in my memory. I tried to escape this maelstrom and lurched upwards out of the scrum, twisting my neck and hearing it click with a loud noise that actually sounded like the word 'click'. My dad, watching from the sidelines, ran onto the pitch, picked me up and took me to Dr Scott and Dr Galvin's surgery. Dr Galvin always dressed in black and looked like he enjoyed listening to be-bop and snapping his fingers. Dr Scott was always more laid back; legend had it that he once visited a patient and spent the whole of the consultation playing snooker with a man who felt dizzy when he stood up and then, after he'd potted the last black, advised him to get to hospital as soon as possible. My dad and I trooped into Dr Scott's consulting room, me walking sideways and looking towards the ceiling like a nun who'd seen a vision. 'Rugby accident?' he asked, and at the time I couldn't fathom how he'd worked that out although later I remembered I was still wearing my kit.

He glanced cursorily at my neck and then said briskly, as though he'd rather be playing snooker with a potential stroke victim, 'this will probably hurt.' I don't like it when doctors say that; I'd rather they lied and said 'You won't feel a thing'. He lifted me up by my neck and swung me like a pub sign in a breeze. He was right. A woman walking down the path to the surgery, saw me flailing, shook her head and turned back. She'd go and get some corn plasters from the chemist. There was a member of the Poorly Folk in the chair.

One last thing. There was always a dog with three legs somewhere in any pit village; one wandered round Darfield for years, defying us to laugh at it, maintaining an air of dignity and exquisite, unfathomable sadness. I thought about it as Doctor Scott hung me. It didn't help.

BUYING CLOTHES

From the vantage point of my early stroll I can look across the Dearne Valley to the huge ASOS warehouse that sits on the edge of Grimethorpe and Great Houghton in the lee of the old pitstack by the four huge windmills that are more a windsmallholding than a

windfarm. The letters stand for As Seen On Screen and, day and night, huge wagons roll out of the gates to deliver clothing to people who, only hours before, were hunched over a screen looking at shirts and wondering if they'd fit in XL or XXL. There's a constantly glowing red sign on the warehouse that announces XPOLOGISTICS to which some wag on Twitter added the word Supercalifragilistic.

The warehouse tells you a little about the complex relationship many Barnsley males have with the buying and wearing of clothes. Many of us feel uncomfortable with buying them. Many of us, let's be honest, allowed our mams to buy them for us for more years than we should have done. When I was at school one of my mates expressed the almost Stalinist view that we should all dress the same, in dark boiler suits and although I expressed surprise at the notion, quite a large percentage of me thought it was a good idea. To understand Barnsley men, as I've tried to do for years and tried to partially articulate in the writing of this book, is often a matter of fathoming their attitude to clothes. A few, like Jud in *Kes*, are dandies, looking, as an assistant in Burton's once said to me, 'as natty as a carrot' in their sharp suits and ties. Many, like me, are blokes who simply don't know what they want to look like and who, even before the days of ubiquitous body-imaging and angels with six-packs on the covers of health magazines staring at you from newsagents' shelves, thought that their necks were too bulbous and their legs were too short. Maybe, if this book is dedicated to anybody, it's dedicated to them.

And it really strikes me, on my stroll, that the click 'n' deliver ethos has saved me from the endless embarrassment of visiting clothes shops that has blighted me since I was a youth. Now I can send off for clothes and, if I don't like them, I can send them back rather than shoving them in the wardrobe. My legs and my neck and my belly and the fact that one of my ears is further up or down (depending which ear you're looking at) than the other on my head doesn't matter anymore. But in the past those things have mattered, oh they've mattered.

My memory map of buying clothes in Barnsley is an endless jumble and tangle of standing in shops sweating profusely and suffering a jacket-based panic attack as pencil thin men or female assistants who looked like somebody's sophisticated older sister looked at you as though you were something that had fallen through a hole in the ceiling from the unoccupied flat above. For the nervous lad like me, it was always better to buy something from the market in Barnsley or Wombwell. Wombwell was easier to get to, but you might see someone you knew. And seeing somebody you know was almost worse than buying the clothes.

I once, in the heady 1960s, as the barricades were going up all over Paris, bought a matching pink paisley shirt and tie on a stall in Wombwell Market. I held it up to the light and it was a psychedelic sunrise. I imagined, wrongly, that it made me look louche. At home I tried it on and my dad said I looked like a spiv, which was his reaction to anything that wasn't office wear. Mind you, in the 1960s they were starting to wear pink paisley shirts in the office, although maybe not in Barnsley. I strutted around in the bedroom pretending I was in the Kinks.

The next day, at school, I was chatting to the Lads just before we went into Spanish and a girl of my acquaintance came up and said, 'I can let you have that John Steinbeck book back at church on Sunday.' The Lads were aghast. They stared open-mouthed like gargoyles or a Bateman cartoon. 'Church? You go to church?' they chorused. I went dying-star-at-the-edge-of-the-universe red. 'Just to ring the bells, not to talk to God', I mumbled, trying to be elegant and ironic. The girl looked smug. 'See you there on Sunday for Bible study,' she said, smiling and twisting the elegant New Testament knife.

I decided to wear my matching shirt and tie for church that day as an act of rebellion and my fellow churchy teenagers murmured their appreciation. The tie sat and hid on the shirt like a cloth chameleon and I'd buttoned the shirt to the top so I couldn't breathe.

After church I stood in the entrance and chatted with the holy girls and boys. Something stirred by the top of the path; shadowy figures rendered anonymous by the sun. They gradually resolved themselves into a group unified only by the fact that they were laughing their heads off, weeping huge tears and shaking their shoulders apocalyptically. Of course it was the Lads. Of course they'd caught early buses and got lifts from parents just to see my coming out of church, like paparazzi hanging around a showbiz wedding.

This was a double humiliation. Not only was I coming out of church behind ladies in hats and blokes in tight suits, I was wearing a pink matching paisley shirt and tie. Even now, forty-odd years later, I'm sweating at the memory as I type and I've had to go and put the kettle on. A couple of years ago I was in a taxi coming home from town and the driver said to me 'Who'd have thought that one day the men of Barnsley would be buying water in bottles and wearing pink shirts?' I didn't say anything but I thought 'Yes, mate, I was a pioneer of the pink shirt. You're driving an early adopter home' but I kept my gob shut.

All through my childhood and early adulthood a man called, at first, Mr Walker, and later Michael Walker, used to come to the house bringing clothes that my mother would buy for a pound a week. He was one of that dying breed, even then in the 1960s, the credit draper, bringing goods to the outskirts (get it?) from his shop in town. I'd see him as I wandered around the village, getting out of his car carrying a pile of cardigans or an octopus of ties. He'd try to wave. Over the years he became a regular Friday fixture and my mother would get his payment card ready, slipping a twenty pound note inside, even though she only paid a pound a week. It was her way of getting change, like people often did in those days, buying a *Daily Mirror* with a note and saying 'I'm just going to crack this tenner.' There was always an element of ritual to the way he gave her, as I remember vividly, three five pound notes and four ones, as though he was the banker in Monopoly. My mother was elegant, and he always brought her elegant clothes; she'd have liked me to be stylish but it was never going to happen. If I wore a suit it looked like I was wearing a suit for a bet. Every so often Mr Walker would bring me a shirt or a jacket or a cardigan and I would dutifully try them on and shake my head and then Mr Walker would take them back. I recall with particular horror, from when I was about ten years old, a pair of brown corduroy lederhosen that my mother and Mr Walker assured me were with it. They didn't say with what, although I suspect they meant with humiliation.

The only item of clothing I ever wore in my teenage years that caused me almost no pain and gave me more than a little pride was my ex-army greatcoat. I bought it from a stall on Barnsley Market and it enveloped me like the political system of the part of the Soviet Union it was meant to have come from. I didn't mind the Lads seeing me in it, and although it was heavy and warm, I would wear it in summer because I thought it made me look like the beat poet I desperately wanted to be. I say the coat almost caused me no pain: the pain it did cause me was the kind of pain that comes with learning a lesson. I was once hitchhiking between Oxford and Cheltenham and, having drunk loads of beer, was desperate for a wee. I dodged behind a skimpy bush and described a liquid arc which was observed by a passing copper and his mate who pulled over with, I thought unnecessary drama, his lights flashing and siren singing. I zipped up quickly and (avert your eyes) messily. 'Hello sir' the taller copper said, his voice dripping with sarcasm from the police college sarcasm seminar. 'You do realise that urinating in a public place carries with it a hefty fine and a possible, if not probable, custodial sentence?' I know now that he was spouting bollocks but at the time I wanted to weep although I thought that if I blubbered he would increase the fine. He looked at the coat. 'Are you a member of the army of the Soviet Union, sir?' he asked, looking at my bright badges. 'No' I said, my voice trembling, 'I'm from Barnsley'.

What happened next more or less justifies this book. He repeated Barnsley with operatic glee, emphasising the 'a' in the word until it almost stretched as far as my intended destination that evening: 'Baaaaaaaaaaaaaaaaaaaaarnsley? Baaaaaaaaaaaaaaaaaaaaarnsley? Well, that's just like the flaming Soviet Union, isn't it? Baaaaaaaaaaaaaaaaarnsley!' and he drove off, laughing. I hope he reads this book. I hope he's joined a branch of the police where he has to wear brown corduroy lederhosen.

BAAAAAAAAAARNSLEY

When I tell people that I'm from Barnsley I suddenly feel like a shepherd in the middle of a field surround by a flock of sheep who think they are the funniest sheep that ever walked the earth on four or two legs. 'I'm from Barnsley' I'll say and the listener will take a deep breath and say 'Baaaaaaaaaaaaaaaaaaarnsley!' holding the 'a' for so long that you fear they might need medical attention. Actually, you don't fear that they might need medical attention: you hope they need medical attention and that it hurts.

Along with the citizens of Wigan and Scunthorpe, but never the inhabitants of Chelsea, Harrogate or Stirling, it's always assumed that people who live in Barnsley are inherently daft and, not to put too fine a point on it, thick. I've not researched this exhaustively but I reckon there must have been a music-hall star years ago called something like Billy Buxton the Babbling Brutalist who did a routine about Wigan, and Scunthorpe, and Baaaaaaarnsley. See: I'm doing it myself now.

When you've lived somewhere all your life your perception of the place is set in stone and everyone else's ideas of the place splash around it as though Barnsley is an island and the world is the sea.

So, just for the record, here are a few ideas about Barnsley that it's easy to debunk. I'll either present the myth as it is, with no comment just to prove how ridiculous it is, or I'll add a little sentence to pop its balloon.

Barnsley is Burnley. No it isn't. Burnley is in Lancashire.

Barnsley is Bardsey. No it isn't. Bardsey is an island.

Barnsley people say 'Eee by gum' and 'Ecky thump' at least once a day for the whole of their lives. No they don't: I'm 61 years old and I promise I've never heard anyone say either of those phrases unless they said them ironically, with inverted commas around them like novelty earrings.

Barnsley people all wear flat caps. Well, some of them do, but their number is shrinking, like the flat caps. It's like any traditional costume, I guess: the older people wear it without thinking, because that's what they've always worn, and the younger people wear it to make a statement about authenticity and rootedness, which is why thousands of Barnsley F.C. fans young and old wore flat caps at Wembley for the Johnstone's Paint Trophy Final in April 2016. It was as though they had been collectively shining a light on a cliché simply to make fun of it. Of course reductionism can work both ways: we played Oxford that day and a line of Tykes sat down and pretended to scull down Wembley way chanting 'You only sing when you're rowing!'

Barnsley is in Gloucestershire. Well, one of them is.

Barnsley people are sentimental. I reckon this idea spread because Barnsley umpire Dickie Bird was often to be seen blubbering at the drop of a catch. I mean the drop of a hat. I'm a sentimental man, too, finding my eyes prickling with tears at Elgar or a minute's silence or a bloke bending down to pick up somebody else's dropped hat. Or dropped catch. Back to the day we played Oxford United at Wembley in 2016 I sat next to man who said 'I get a bit excited, lad'. I said that we all got a bit excited, but I think that by 'excited' he meant 'sentimental'. As the game progressed he kept a running commentary going on the progress of his excitement: 'Time to get the flag out, lad.' 'Time for the shirt off, lad.' I thought that was the end of his excitement, or sentimentality, but the best, the most beautiful, the moment that still moves me when I think about it, was yet to come. The final whistle went and the red and white part of Wembley erupted in cheering. The bloke cheered but then he sank to the ground. He beat the floor with his fists and shouted 'Me dad!' because, I guess, his dad probably took him to matches as a child and couldn't, for whatever reason, take him any more. I was going to ask him but then he stood up, looked me in the eye and said 'Does tha mind if I embrace thi?' I nodded, overcome, and said 'Please do!' He stepped forward. He dropped his flag to the floor. I was expecting a bear-like smothering but he held me at arms length and patted me twice on the back. 'Hey, tha can hug me if tha wants,' I said, employing the demotic. He patted me again. It was like a tiny spider had got inside my shirt. He said a phrase that is pure, pure Barnsley: 'Tha reyt. Tha reyt'; the exact translation is imprecise but it means 'it's all right, my friend, I don't need to do anything else. What I am doing is sufficient for the task in hand: it has a delicate ecology that I don't want to break.' Tha reyt.

Barnsley is a state of mind. Now this is true. Our diaspora is well scattered but still walks the streets of Tarn. I did a gig in Guernsey a few years ago and the organiser said that I'd be met at the airport by a man in a Barnsley shirt, and I was. He stood proudly in the arrivals area wearing a home shirt and holding a BFC scarf. His accent was broader than mine. He talked about Barnsley all the way to the gig. In the interval he talked about Barnsley. On the way to the hotel he talked about Barnsley. He took me to the airport and said he'd see me at Oakwell next month. I think if I'd photographed him with a heat-seeking camera I would have seen him walking along surrounded by scenes from Barnsley rather than the Guernsey beachscape. This is true of all places, I guess, but it seems to me that it's truer in Barnsley (and going back to my earlier point) in Wigan, and Scunthorpe.

Notes

1. Get yourselves down to The Academy Theatre www.theacademytheatre.co.uk
2. Harry Worth should be better known than he is, although it's true that Barnsley people of a certain age can do his shop-window trick (ask your dad). There should be a Harry Worth Appreciation Society. Maybe I'll start one.
3. A Beverley Bar bus was so called because the roof was a distinctive shape, enabling it to drive under the arch in the middle of that East Yorkshire town without scraping the roof off.
4. www.elsecarheritage.com www.elsecarrailway.co.uk
5. The Barnsley, Dearne and Dove Canals Trust website is well worth having a look at. They need volunteers! www.bddct.org.uk
6. Worsbrough Mill Website: www.WorsbroughMill.com
7. Hemingfield Pit's website really is a mine (hoho) of information on all kinds of mining and history in this part of the world. Hemingfieldcolliery.wordpress.com
8. If you want to know more about the wonderful world of bellringing, have a look at the magazine The Ringing World www.ringingworld.co.uk
9. www.wortleyhall.co.uk

AFTERWORD

I'm writing this quite late on a Saturday night; it's dark outside and the whole of Barnsley, real Barnsley, is either settling down for the night or getting ready to go out. I feel squeezed dry, in a good way. I feel that, to paraphrase the song, I've looked at Barnsley from all sides now, from East and West and North and South, and it's Barnsley's illusions I recall, because I really don't know this town at all.

I started this book thinking I was a know-all, and by the end I was a know-nowt. I realised that I knew my home village of Darfield pretty well; I knew Wombwell and I knew Goldthorpe and Thurnscoe and the town centre. I wasn't so sure about Darton or Mapplewell or Penistone, and as far as I knew I'd never been to Carlecotes. Barnsley stretched out in front of me like a picnic or a finger buffet, and I knew that I'd have to take my time and sample the quiche as well as the pork pie.

Writing this book has opened my eyes to the place I've lived in all my life, and I hope it'll open your eyes too. It's made me look at the town as a visitor might, and I hope that you'll come and see us and use this book as a guide. I know I will.

There are certain repeating tropes that have floated to the surface again and again as I've been writing this book, and I think it's worth going through them again in order to prove that there is truth in a cliché, almost as though one is an anagram of the other.

So: Barnsley Borough is more than just the town and the town centre; it's the town centre and a lot of villages, each one with its own history and idiosyncrasies. There are certain things that remain the same, though: each village was rural once. In most of the villages there was a big house that could have been demolished or turned into flats or a care home or fallen into ruin or being part of a regeneration project. In most of the villages the pits arrived and completely changed the landscape. Streets and shops and schools and transport systems grew up very quickly and they form the basis of the villages you see today. Churches are important to the journey of this book, sometimes because they were sometimes the oldest building in the village and sometimes because they were built with coal money and they reflected the wealth that was being generated round here.

Coal reigned supreme in this part of the world: the getting of it scarred the land and populated it. It left huge muckstacks all over the place and there was pithead gear everywhere you looked. People came from all over the country to work here, and their languages and dialects soaked into the ways of speech round here, making a Barnsley tongue that is at once harsh and loving, brusque and poetic.

And then the pits went: in the space of a decade, more or less, they were wiped from the face of the map and the town changed forever. Whole communities were left to rot, and each of them responded in their own way, and now, as I write this, each of them is pulling itself up from the mud to the stars; slowly, slowly.

The Barnsley that I'm encouraging you to visit is still living through this aftermath, still trying to reinvent itself, still trying to gaze nervously forward as it looks hesitantly backwards. When you visit it you'll get the sense that the dust of history hasn't quite settled, that we're still rubbing our eyes and blinking.

Come and see us. Come and help us see.

GLOSSARY

Snooerman: snowman
Termarter: tomato
Deead: dead
Balloinz: balloons
Slairin: sliding
Zizzin: sleeping
Pepper's: Larratt Pepper's bus company
Leeter: lighter
Sumbdy: somebody
Vesser: vest
Leet: light
Neet: night
Semmas: same as
Shoorts: shorts
Allared: allowed
Lickle: little

THE PHOTOGRAPHS

* Photograph by Peter Finch

THE AUTHOR

Ian McMillan is the poet, journalist, playwright, and broadcaster known as the 'Bard of Barnsley'. He began performing in the 1970s and has published several collections of poetry, for adults and children. He is an enthusiastic advocate of poetry, and hosts the *The Verb*, and Proms variation *Adverb*, on Radio 3, 'dedicated to investigating spoken words around the globe'.

McMillan has had journalism published in *Q* magazine and *Mojo*, and writes a weekly column for *The Barnsley Chronicle*. He is also 'poet in residence' to Barnsley F.C. His play *Sister Josephine Kicks the Habit* premiered in 2005, and in 2010 McMillan was appointed poet-in-residence at the English National Opera. He is a roving contributor to Radio 4's the *Today Programme*, and has also been a panelist on *Just A Minute* and was a castaway on *Desert Island Discs*. He is a frequent guest on *Newsnight Review*, *The Mark Radcliffe Show*, *You & Yours*, *The Culture Show*, *Never Mind The Full Stops* and *Have I Got News For You?*, and narrated *The Museum* on BBC 2. He has also provided voice-overs in tv advertisements.

In 2007, McMillan published *Collins Chelp and Chunter: a Guide to the Tyke*, and his *Neither Nowt Nor Summat: In search of the meaning of Yorkshire* was published in 2015. He lives in Darfield, the town of his birth.

INDEX

Other Titles in the series

SEREN

Well chosen words

Seren is an independent publisher with a wide-ranging list which includes poetry, fiction, biography, art, translation, criticism and history. Many of our books and authors have been on longlists and shortlists for – or won – major literary prizes, among them the Costa Award, the Jerwood Fiction Uncovered Prize, the Man Booker, the Desmond Elliott Prize, The Writers' Guild Award, Forward Prize and TS Eliot Prize.

At the heart of our list is a beautiful poem, a good story told well or an idea or history presented interestingly or provocatively. We're international in authorship and readership though our roots are here in Wales (Seren means Star in Welsh), where we prove that writers from a small country with an intricate culture have a worldwide relevance.

Our aim is to publish work of the highest literary and artistic merit that also succeeds commercially in a competitive, fast changing environment. You can help us achieve this goal by reading more of our books – available from all good bookshops and increasingly as e-books. You can also buy them at 20% discount from our website, and get monthly updates about forthcoming titles, readings, launches and other news about Seren and the authors we publish.

www.serenbooks.com